W9-AYM-517

INDIANS, COWBOYS, and FARMERS

and the Battle for the Great Plains

1865–1910

★★ *The Drama of* AMERICAN HISTORY ★★

INDIANS, COWBOYS, and FARMERS

and the Battle for the Great Plains

1865–1910

Christopher Collier
James Lincoln Collier

BENCHMARK BOOKS

MARSHALL CAVENDISH
NEW YORK

ACKNOWLEDGMENT: The authors wish to thank Elliott West, Professor of History, University of Arkansas, for his careful reading of the text of this volume in The Drama of American History series and his thoughtful and useful comments. The work has been much improved by Professor West's notes. The authors are deeply in his debt, but, of course, assume full responsibility for the substance of the work, including any errors that may appear.

Photo research by James Lincoln Collier.
cover photo: Courtesy of the Sid Richardson Collection of Western Art
PICTURE CREDITS: The photographs in this book are used by permission and through the courtesy of: New York Public Library: 10, 11, 15, 16 (top & bottom), 18, 20, 23, 52, 59, 60 (bottom), 71, 74; Sid Richardson Collection of Western Art, Fort Worth, Texas: 26, 44, 45; The National Archives: 28, 36; Corbis/Bettmann: 31, 32, 33, 76, 79, 80, 81, 85, 87 (bottom); Corbis/Bettmann - UPI: 89; Amon Carter Museum, Fort Worth, Texas: 46, 48, 66; California State Railroad Museum, Sacramento: 60 (top).

Benchmark Books
Marshall Cavendish Corporation
99 White Plains Road
Tarrytown, New York 10591-9001

©2001 Christopher Collier and James Lincoln Collier

Library of Congress Cataloging-in-Publication Data
Collier, Christopher, 1930-
Indians, cowboys, and farmers and the battle for the Great Plains,1865-1910 /
by Christopher Collier and James Lincoln Collier.
p. cm.
Includes bibliographical references and index.
Summary: Discusses the settling of the area between the Missouri River and the Rocky Mountains and the con-flicting interests of the different groups involved—the Indians, cowboys, farmers, sheepherders, and railroad barons.
ISBN 0-7614-1052-X
1. Indians of North America—Wars—Great Plains—Juvenile literature. 2. Indians of North America—Land tenure—Great Plains--Juvenile literature. 3. Frontier and pioneer life—Great Plains—HistoryvJuvenile literature. 4. Great Plains—Social life and customs—Juvenile literature.

[1. Great Plains—History. 2. Frontier and pioneer life—Great Plains—History. 3. Indians of North America—Great Plains.]   I. Collier, James Lincoln, 1928- II. Title.
E78.G73 C55 2000
978'.02—dc21
00-021103

Printed in the United States of America
1 3 5 6 4 2

CONTENTS

PREFACE

Over many years of both teaching and writing for students at all levels, from grammar school to graduate school, it has been borne in on us that many, if not most, American history textbooks suffer from trying to include everything of any moment in the history of the nation. Students become lost in a swamp of factual information, and as a consequence lose track of how those facts fit together and why they are significant and relevant to the world today.

In this series, our effort has been to strip the vast amount of available detail down to a central core. Our aim is to draw in bold strokes, providing enough information, but no more than is necessary, to bring out the basic themes of the American story, and what they mean to us now. We believe that it is surely more important for students to grasp the underlying concepts and ideas that emerge from the movement of history, than to memorize an array of facts and figures.

The difference between this series and many standard texts lies in what has been left out. We are convinced that students will better remember the important themes if they are not buried under a heap of names, dates, and places.

In this sense, our primary goal is what might be called citizenship education. We think it is critically important for America as a nation and Americans as individuals to understand the origins and workings of the public institutions that are central to American society. We have asked ourselves again and again what is most important for citizens of our democracy to know so they can most effectively make the system work for them and the nation. For this reason, we have focused on political and institutional history, leaving social and cultural history less well developed.

This series is divided into volumes that move chronologically through the American story. Each is built around a single topic, such as the Pilgrims, the Constitutional Convention, or immigration. Each volume has been written so that it can stand alone, for students who wish to research a given topic. As a consequence, in many cases material from previous volumes is repeated, usually in abbreviated form, to set the topic in its historical context. That is to say, students of the Constitutional Convention must be given some idea of relations with England, and why the Revolution was fought, even though the material was covered in detail in a previous volume. Readers should find that each volume tells an entire story that can be read with or without reference to other volumes.

Despite our belief that it is of the first importance to outline sharply basic concepts and generalizations, we have not neglected the great dramas of American history. The stories that will hold the attention of students are here, and we believe they will help the concepts they illustrate to stick in their minds. We think, for example, that knowing of Abraham Baldwin's brave and dramatic decision to vote with the small states at the Constitutional Convention will bring alive the Connecticut Compromise, out of which grew the American Senate.

Each of these volumes has been read by esteemed specialists in its particular topic; we have benefited from their comments.

CHAPTER I

Before the White Man

The settling of the American West is a classic story that has captured the imagination of people everywhere. Even while it was going on, stories of cowboys and Indians were being read by boys and girls in England and Russia as well as the United States. Some of the most famous of all movies, like *Shane* and *High Noon*, draw on this great romantic story. "Cowboy" songs, like "Bury Me Not on the Lone Prairie," are still sung by Americans. The heroes of this story, like Buffalo Bill, Geronimo, Wild Bill Hickok, Sitting Bull, and George Armstrong Custer, are as well known to us as biblical names or the heroes of our Revolution.

Needless to say, much of what we learn from stories and movies is myth and legend. Still, when the legends are peeled away, the story of the contest for the West among Indians, cowboys, sheepherders, railroad barons, ranchers, and farmers is filled with high drama. That dramatic story is the subject of this book.

Actually, when we speak of the "West" in this manner, we are really talking about the area known as the Great Plains, which lies, roughly, between the Missouri River and the Rocky Mountains. The lands farther west, including the present states of New Mexico, Arizona, California,

Washington, and Oregon, have different stories. (We have told the story of California and the Southwest in the volume in this series called *Hispanic America, California, Texas and the Mexican War, 1835–1850.*) This story, then, is about the battle for the Great Plains.

One of the most startling aspects of this fascinating story is the speed with which it happened, once it got started. It took the early English settlers 150 years to move from the Atlantic Coast across the Alleghenies, some two hundred miles. Movement was even slower in the Far West: The first Spanish explorers reached Lower California in 1533, but not until 1769 did the Spanish make any real effort to colonize the region. (The story of the Indians' encounter with the Spanish is told in the volume in this series called *Hispanic America.*)

The Spanish explorer Francisco de Coronado encountered Quiviran Indians (later known as Wichita) along the Arkansas River in 1541, but the Great Plains, too, remained unexploited by Europeans for centuries, though French and English traders and trappers had been active along

This engraving of any army encampment by the Cheyenne River in South Dakota suggests the vast emptiness of the Great Plains.

One of the greatest Western legends was William Cody, who as "Buffalo Bill" toured the world with a western show featuring trick shooting, riding, and roping. His show owed more to imagination than actuality, and was important in building the folklore of the West.

the upper Missouri River since before the American Revolution in the 1770s. When Americans began to flood into the area in about 1850, however, they filled it so rapidly that in 1890 the director of the U.S. census announced that any clear frontier line was gone. To give a couple of examples, in 1860 the population of Nebraska was 60,000; by 1890 it was over a million. In Iowa the population density in 1860 was four times what it had been in 1850. Indeed, more land was taken up between 1870 and 1900 than in the entire history of European settlement in America before 1870—about 250 years.

To understand this astonishing event we need to know something about the climate and geography of the area. The vast central part of North America between the Allegheny mountain range and the Rocky Mountains is essentially a great treeless region, flat in some places, rolling hills in others, broken here and there by smaller mountain ranges, rivers, lakes, and other features. However, this prairie land is not the same everywhere. The key is rainfall. Generally speaking, moisture is picked up from oceans and carried over land by winds. In the east, rain has usu-

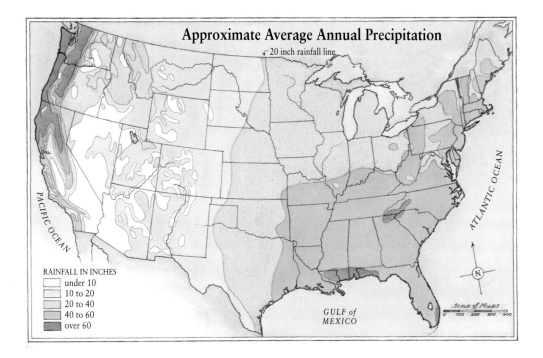

Approximate Average Annual Precipitation

20 inch rainfall line

PACIFIC OCEAN

ATLANTIC OCEAN

GULF of MEXICO

RAINFALL IN INCHES
- under 10
- 10 to 20
- 20 to 40
- 40 to 60
- over 60

N

SCALE of MILES
0   100   200   300   400

ally been plentiful: The eastern United States has only occasionally suffered from a prolonged drought. However, water-bearing winds from the Pacific Ocean run into the Sierra Nevada Mountains and then the Rockies. For technical reasons, these mountains force most of the rain out of the Pacific winds, leaving a "rain shadow" on the eastern side of the Rockies that reaches inland for hundreds of miles. Roughly speaking, the 100th meridian marks the eastern boundary of the Great Plains; to the east, rain averages over 20 inches a year; to the west, fewer.

Before the arrival of the Europeans, the land to the east was covered almost entirely with forest. To the west, under the rain shadow, the plains were treeless, except along the few rivers that cut through it. Tall grass, in some cases as much as five or six feet high that grew east of the 100th meridian, became shorter to the west. These great fields of grass, stretching for hundreds of miles in all directions, encouraged the growth of huge herds of grass-eating animals, particularly pronghorn antelopes and buffalo, which roamed by the millions across the vast grassland.

But if the land was hospitable to these big grazing animals, it was less so to human beings. Strong winds could blow for days at a time. Temperatures would rise to 110 degrees or more in the summer, drop to 20 or 30 degrees below zero in the winter and fluctuate as much as 60 degrees in a single day: One historian has noted changes of 100 degrees in twenty-four hours. The shadeless, monotonous plains had none of the pleasant views of lakes, hills, or woods to be found in the east. For the farmers to come, the tough, matted turf, with its thick root system, was very difficult to plough for cultivation. Indeed, earlier American explorers, noting the absence of trees, called much of this region "the Great American Desert."

The Plains were not all of a piece. Moisture from the Gulf of Mexico gave the southern part of it, principally Texas, more rainfall than reached the Dakotas. From the western tip of the Great Lakes to the Rio Grande and from the Mississippi River to the Rockies, the Great Plains exhibited great variation in topography and climate. But for human beings walking across it, the change was so gradual the landscape seemed monotonously the same. As one historian has written about the high Plains, ". . . travelers were impressed by what was *not* there, the sheer immensity of unbroken sweep."

Yet despite everything, human beings lived there—lived very well in their own terms. When we think of Indians of lore and legend, of movies and books, it is not the Indians of the East with their cornfields and fishing nets, nor those of the Northwest chasing whales in oversized canoes, whom we see in our minds. Instead, it is the Indians of the Great Plains dashing across the prairie on their wiry ponies; the Indians who wore feathered headdresses and buffalo robes. How many of them there were on the Plains is not certain, but they certainly numbered in the tens of thousands.

The Plains culture of the Indians was established within relatively recent times. When the Spanish arrived at the Plains area in the 1500s

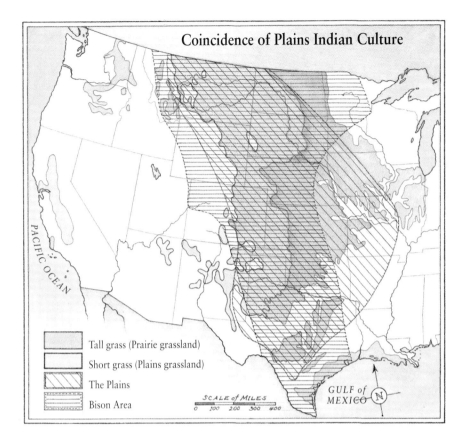

Coincidence of Plains Indian Culture

PACIFIC OCEAN

Tall grass (Prairie grassland)
Short grass (Plains grassland)
The Plains
Bison Area

SCALE of MILES
0   100   200   300   400

GULF of
MEXICO   N

they came on horseback. After the Pueblo Revolt of 1580 (see the volume *Hispanic America*), horses were stolen and traded by Indians. Some horses were found running wild on the Plains, feeding on the abundant grass as the buffalo did. The Indians learned to tame them, and became expert horsemen, riding bareback instead of on saddles as the Europeans did. A rider has considerable advantages over someone on foot, both in fighting and in hunting large game like buffalo. Soon most of the Plains Indians had adopted the horse culture. The adoption of the horse culture upset traditional territorial arrangements, and a great many tribal battles arose out of conflicting claims to the same buffalo-rich prairie grassland.

Now the Indians were able to slaughter buffalo and other game almost at will. The buffalo was a great source of wealth. Its meat was tasty and nourishing. Its hide could be made into robes, moccasins,

This painting by the famous western artist George Catlin shows a typical Assiniboin encampment, with tepees made of skins, naked children, a bareback rider, and a "travois" pulled by a dog, a common Indian method of transporting goods about the prairie.

tepees, and much else. Its sinews provided cord and bowstrings. Its dung, usually called "buffalo chips," could be burned as fuel. With massive herds of buffalo and other animals everywhere around them, the Plains Indians became one of the wealthiest groups, in Indian terms, on the North American continent. They made elaborate costumes for themselves, and they had plenty of leisure for ceremonies and games.

They also had the time and energy for warfare, a necessary occupation since the new horse culture brought territorial expansion and competition for resources such as water and buffalo. To most of the Plains

Left: Many of the pictures in this chapter were painted by George Catlin, an artist who became passionate about the Indian West at an early age, and was determined to capture it in paint before it disappeared. Despite years of work and many fine paintings, he did not achieve financial success in his time, but today he is honored for preserving the ancient Indian lifestyle. Here he shows himself painting a portrait of an Indian warrior in a camp on the Plains.

Below: The culture of the Plains Indians grew up around the buffalo, especially after the Indians acquired horses from the Spanish. On horseback the Indians could kill far more buffalo than they needed, and as a consequence lived prosperous lives, in Indian terms.

Indians, as well as many other Indians elsewhere, war was seen as a challenge, a way to achieve fame and glory. As one authority has written, Plains Indians lived "in a society where a man's career and standing depended on his military prowess." Bravery in battle was highly prized. Best was to strike an enemy without killing him or getting hit yourself; or to steal his weapons. These daring exploits were called a *coup*. Leaders were often chosen from battle heroes. Indeed, Indian women sometimes fought in battle, although that was rare; most Indian women disliked the wars, which often took their sons and husbands. One said, "We women sometimes tried to keep our men from going to war, but this was like talking to winter winds. Always some man was missing, and always some woman was having to go and live with her relatives . . . It was no good." Yet women, too, sometimes encouraged war, for they preferred war heroes for husbands, and told their sons to be brave in battle.

For young Indian men, war was an essential part of life. They could not win respect through success in business, sports, or scholarship; for most it had to be in battle. And even when tribal elders counseled against fighting, the young men would often go off on a raid on their own because, as one old woman explained, "they could not marry until they had counted coup. . . . " We need to bear this in mind; for clearly when the whites began to move onto the Great Plains there was no possibility that the Indians would simply retreat.

Indeed, constant warfare among Indians over long periods of time generated so much hatred that tribes would not join together to defend against white men; often one tribe would join the whites against long-term rival Indians. Even today, it is often said among them, "The worst enemy of an Indian is another Indian." This lack of unity helps explain why Indians ultimately lost their lands to Europeans all the way from New England to California and from Mexico through Canada.

In addition to conflicts over territory, there had always been a market for slaves, which was expanded after the Spanish arrived, and tribes warred against one another to take captives to sell into slavery. "Apaches," writes one historian, "relied on human captives as a valuable commodity to supplement their trade in bison meat and skins."

It is not inaccurate to call the Plains Indians—at least the men—a "warlike" people. Though, as one close observer has said, "They governed themselves by highly democratic political systems in which the leader carried out the will of the people. . . . With some notable exceptions, they exalted war and bestowed great prestige on the successful warrior. They cherished freedom, independence, and dignity of the indi-

Warfare among Indian tribes was constant, as much a way of life among them as the buffalo hunt. This picture by another famous western artist, Charles M. Russell, shows members of Blackfeet and Sioux tribes battling. By the early nineteenth century the Plains Indians had acquired guns from the whites.

vidual, the family, and the group." This highly individualistic culture made it very difficult for tribal elders to control spirited young men determined to make their mark through military adventure. Thus, long before the arrival of Europeans, Indians were battling each other.

The arena for the battle of Plains between American whites and Indians was laid in 1803, when President Thomas Jefferson bought from France the area known as the Louisiana Purchase, a huge funnel-shaped piece of land running from Louisiana up into the Dakotas that doubled the size of the United States. Americans knew little about this land, and in 1804 Jefferson sent the famous Lewis and Clark expedition through the Great Plains to the mouth of the Columbia River in what is today the state of Washington to find out what was there, and if possible discover a water route to the Pacific. Other expeditions, such as that of Zebulon Pike's across the southern Plains and the Rocky Mountains, followed and soon it was clear that the Great Plains, although promising, was a hard land. There was no immediate rush to settle it. (The story of the Lewis and Clark expedition is told in the volume called *Jeffersonian Republicans* in this series.)

Nonetheless, there were pressures on Americans in the East to look westward. American population was growing rapidly, due both to high birth rates and immigration; the soil, especially in the long-settled areas along the Atlantic Coast, was being depleted of essential minerals.

In 1846 England and the United States agreed to divide the great Northwest and what became the states of Washington, Oregon, and Idaho were clear of international rivalries and were open for white Americans to settle. Then, in 1848, the United States, as a result of the Mexican War, acquired the land that would become the states of Utah, Arizona, and California, and parts of New Mexico and Colorado. America now stretched from sea to shining sea, and it was clear that the Great Plains would have to be absorbed into the nation somehow. For a second matter, in 1848 gold was discovered in California. By the next year easterners were streaming across the Great Plains by the tens of thousands, mostly in trains of the famous covered wagons, but sometimes on foot with packs on their backs, or even pushing wheelbarrows containing meager belongings. The national government encouraged this "westering" movement: Hispanics and Indians were still a major presence in California. Clearly, the best way to hold the Far West for America was to fill it with Americans. And now the conflict between Indians and white Americans for the Great Plains began to heat up.

The Sioux, whom we focus on here, were typical of all the Plains Indians; on the southern Plains Cheyennes and Arapahos shared the horse and buffalo culture as well. Farther south, the Comanches "succeeded in fusing horse and rider and in carrying the horse and buffalo

culture to the peak of refinement." They were referred to as "The Lords of the Plains," and the artist George Catlin described them in the 1830s as "the most extraordinary horsemen that I have yet seen in my travels, and I doubt . . . whether any people in the world can surpass them."

Indian males, even as boys, took pride in their ability to endure any amount of pain and hardship. In this Catlin picture, two young men have hung themselves from their skin to show that they can endure the pain in silence.

For generations these Indians had been fighting each other over territorial limits, access to buffalo herds and water, and matters of insult and honor. Now they had more powerful intruders to fight.

Attitudes of European settlers in America toward the Indians they found there were, right from the beginning, mixed. Furthermore, these attitudes changed over time. At first the idea was that Indians would quickly see the advantages of European culture, with its metal tools and weapons, large houses, and rich agriculture, and would adopt the European lifestyle. But as much as Indians liked European hoes, knives, kettles, and guns, they also preferred their own way of life, and although some did adopt European ways, most resisted. Slowly they were driven westward, at first over the Alleghenies, and then bit by bit toward the Mississippi. (The 17th-century Indian-European contact is described in the volume called *Clash of Cultures* in this series.)

By the 1830s a new idea had become prevalent among white Americans: The Indians should be placed on their own special territories, called "reservations," where they could live as they liked—or more accurately, as hostile climate, topography, and soil would permit—and, not incidentally, leave the rest of the land to whites. One result was that in the 1830s large numbers of Southeastern Indians were driven across the Mississippi into Kansas and other areas, where inevitably they came into conflict with the Plains Indians. And before 1848 it was generally believed by most whites that the Indians could have the Great Plains, this Great American Desert.

But now, with the acquisition of the Far West by the United States and massive migrations across the Plains by gold seekers to California in 1849 and Colorado ten years later, everything was changed. The "overlanders," inevitably, chose the best routes across the prairies, regardless of government agreements with the Indians, or Indian wishes. They trampled down the grass, and frightened off the game. The Indians were disturbed, but there was still plenty of land, and they did not fight back;

despite legends of encircled wagon trains fighting off mounted warriors, the overlanders saw Indians only infrequently and rarely had to fight them. The best estimates are that more Indians than whites were killed, and only about one-tenth of 1 percent of the overlanders of the 1850s died at the hands of Indians.

But by the 1850s Americans were beginning to realize that the northern Great Plains could be successfully farmed after all. In particular, this vast grassland was eminently suitable for livestock like sheep and cattle. Whites began simply moving onto the Plains and settling themselves there, regardless of the laws.

One of the great problems for the Indians was that U.S. government policy toward them was confused, contradictory, and frequently changed. Furthermore, a great many Americans had always ignored government policy, illegally settling on Indian lands, or trading with them, equally illegally. Probably the majority of Americans, as well as government officials, wished that the Indians would just go away. But of course the Indians were not about to do that. The result was that again and again Americans would take matters into their own hands, as the overlanders and early settlers on the Plains did. The government wished to see this land settled, and turned a blind eye to these incursions into Indian land. Eventually, as these situations got out of control, the United States would negotiate with the Indians once again, forcing this or that group of Indians to give up part of the territory previously guaranteed to them, or even making them once again relocate farther west—and often not for the last time.

Regrettably, there were some Americans both inside the government and out of it who were willing to see the Indians exterminated. Such people were probably a small minority, and few would admit to it, but even among high government officials the attitude that the only good Indian was a dead Indian did exist. Indeed the commanding general of the U.S. Army in 1881, William Tecumseh Sherman, said, "The Indian must make room for the white man, move away ahead of him, or learn his ways and settle down beside him, else a war of extermination must follow."

After the close of the Civil War in 1865, then, the Indians were being forced onto reservations, some of them quite small, others containing thousands of square miles of land. It was hard enough for the Indians, especially the Plains Indians, to give up their roving lifestyle; to make matters worse, over the years the federal government more and more insisted that Indians adopt white ways. On some reservations Indian men were required to cut their long hair, a matter of pride with them. They were encouraged to wear European clothing, to farm instead of hunt, even forbidden to practice their traditional religious dances and other

Life for the Plains Indians, however, was not all pain and hardship. Here two groups of Indians play a ball game similar to lacrosse, from which the modern lacrosse was derived. This is another Catlin painting.

ceremonies. Said one Lakota, "The white people wish to make us cause the spirits of our dead to be ashamed."

In 1836 the federal government had established its Bureau of Indian Affairs to enforce Indian policy and manage the reservations. As the reservation system expanded after the 1860s, the agents of the Bureau in effect ran the lives of the Indians there. The agent was supposed to distribute money to Indians owed them by treaty agreements, encourage them to adopt white ways, and protect them from whites intent on preying on them. In particular, the agent was to prevent whites from selling the Indians whiskey. Liquor had been a problem for many Indians for some time, but, demoralized by defeat by whites, more of them turned to whiskey for solace.

Unfortunately, many of the Indian agents proved to be corrupt. They siphoned off huge amounts of the money meant for the Indians, they joined in cahoots with the whiskey dealers, they sold for their own profit tools, blankets, and other goods intended for the Indians. Few government offices have been as corrupt as the Bureau of Indian Affairs was in the second half of the nineteenth century. And those who were not dishonest were overworked, understaffed, lonely, bored, and frustrated.

Under unremitting pressure to give up tribal ways, many Indians capitulated. Some simply lost all spirit and drifted. Some of the men joined reservation constabulary forces, put on military uniforms, and helped to police their own people. But some of them were determined to fight back.

CHAPTER II

The Flames of War Rise Higher

The Indian wars of the period 1861 through the 1890s cannot be fit into a neat scheme. Fighting broke out sporadically, usually, but not always, when some Indians tried to maintain elements of their culture of traditional hunting grounds contrary to orders from whites, or tried to prevent settlers or cattlemen from encroaching on their land, or refused to stay on reservations they had been forcibly confined to.

Complicating matters were the wars of conquest Indians had long been involved in among themselves. In the northern part of the Great Plains, the Western Sioux (sometimes called the Lakotas) and their allies, the Eastern Sioux and the Cheyennes, had been fighting other tribes there and had taken over large portions of the Plains where the buffalo roamed. In the south, the Comanches had been at war with various of the tribes around them and had become dominant in the area. Wars of conquest of this kind were frequent among the Indians, as indeed they have been and continue to be among Europeans, Africans, and most other peoples.

A particularly serious problem for the Indians was the decimation of the buffalo. The animal was central to the existence of the Plains Indians.

Warfare among the Indians was sometimes a kind of deadly sport, engaged in for reasons of prestige and revenge; more often the motive was territorial control. In this picture by Charles Russell an Indian is attempting to "count coup"—that is, touch an enemy with a stick without actually killing him. An Indian warrior got great prestige from counting coup.

It was their main source of food, clothing, shelter, fuel, and many other things. The buffalo, indeed, was not just a commodity, but for many Indians carried religious significance.

There once had been at least 25 million buffalo on the Great Plains, plenty enough for the Indians. But as the whites began to flood onto the Plains, the Indians discovered that they could trade buffalo hides for guns, knives, and metal objects. The best robes were made of the skins of female buffalo killed in the winter when the fur was thickest. Each year Indians slaughtered up to 100,000 mostly female buffalo for the fur trade, leaving the meat to rot on the Plains. And, of course, with fewer females in the herd, there would be fewer buffalo calves the next spring.

The whites crossing the Plains killed buffalo for food or even for sport; but the real damage the American pioneers did was to disrupt the herds of lumbering creatures and to drive them from portions of their range. Natural factors, too, were hurting the buffalo. During the mid-nineteenth century, periods of drought affected their food supply. Disease brought in by cattle also hurt the buffalo. It is probable that these bad breaks of nature were at least as much responsible for the decline of the buffalo as were man-made causes. Then, in 1871, a new process for curing hides was developed that permitted the use of buffalo skin for manufacturing uses. Professional buffalo hunters, equipped with high-powered rifles, swept the Plains, slaughtering buffalo in incredible numbers, as many as a million a year. They took the hides and left the bodies to rot, so that at times the Plains would stink for miles around. The coming of the transcontinental railroad was also an important factor. Not only did the railroad trains disrupt the environment but they allowed buffalo hunters an easy way to ship mountains of hides back east. (See Chapter Four for more on railroads.)

So the buffalo died out. From 10 million in the middle of the century they rapidly dwindled, until by the 1880s the buffalo was almost extinct, and would have died out altogether except for the work of a few dedicated conservationists. These efforts succeeded: In the year 2000 there were perhaps 125,000 buffalo in the United States and nearly as many in Canada.

The decimation of the buffalo was by itself enough to have drastically changed life for the Plains Indians. But there was more. By the 1860s the U.S. government, in order to encourage white settlement of the West generally, had built strings of forts across the Plains, and had garrisoned troops in them, about 20 percent of them were African-Americans, some freed from slavery by the Civil War. The Indians called them "buffalo soldiers" because, according to one account, the soldiers' curly hair reminded them of buffalo coats—a term of respect, of course, because Indians

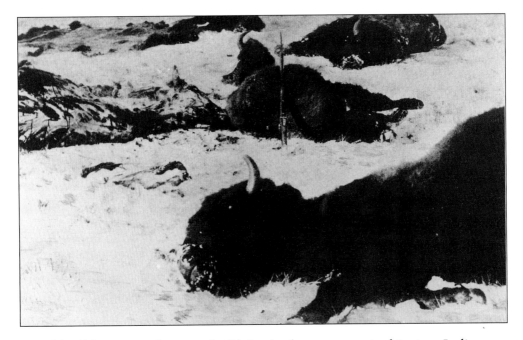

Dead buffalo scattered across the Plains in the snow await skinning. Indians killed a large number of buffalo for skins to trade with whites, but greater damage was done by whites in the time after the railroads came, when it was easier to transport skins east.

so admired the strength and stamina of the buffalo. These troops—white and black—were there to aid the overlanders in various ways, and to protect them from Indians if necessary.

By the 1860s the Sioux had grown to resent the presence of whites on lands the Sioux felt they themselves owned by right of conquest over other Indians. In one perhaps typical incident, an Indian butchered a cow belonging to whites. U.S. soldiers came to the Indian village and the Sioux agreed to pay for the cow, but the soldiers shot the chief who had negotiated the price. In turn the Indians killed all the soldiers, and the war began to heat up. As is always the case in war, once it gets started emotions rise higher and higher, and it inevitably runs out of control.

Retaliation was answered with retaliation, with both whites and Indians killing women and children as well as warriors. Over the years of the 1860s and 1870s many battles between white soldiers and the Sioux and their allies were fought. The Indians won some of them, the whites some. A lot of blood was shed, and a lot of bitterness was created on both sides.

The Sioux, however, were not alone in fighting the whites. One well-known fight involved the famous Chief Joseph and his followers from the Nez Percé Indians of the Northwest. Chief Joseph had led his people onto a reservation in the Wallowa Valley, where there were also Christian Nez Percé farmers. But local settlers wanted this valuable piece of land, and persuaded the government to reduce the size of the reservation. After some young Nez Percé warriors killed some white settlers and the troops sent to punish them, Joseph and other chiefs decided to move away. Six hundred and fifty Nez Percé men, women, and children began a flight for freedom, pursued by hundreds of soldiers in several columns. The Nez Percé hid in valleys, in the woods, in the mountains. From time to time U.S. troops found them, and every time the Nez Percé defeated the soldiers in battle.

Still, the Nez Percé were badly outnumbered. They sought refuge with the Crow Indians in the northern Plains, but discovered that the Crows were being hired as scouts by the American soldiers. They turned north, hoping to escape into Canada. Forty miles short of the border the American soldiers caught them and surrounded them. Most of the warrior leaders were killed, but for five days in bitter cold Joseph held out, watching his people suffer and die, and then he and the other chiefs gave up. Chief Joseph did not speak English, but he is reported to have said something like, "Hear me, my chiefs, I am tired; my heart is sick and sad. From where the sun now stands, I will fight no more forever."

The description of the wars against the Sioux and Nez Percé on the northern Plains illustrates what was going on also farther south. There the Cheyennes, Kiowas, and Comanches, among others, were struggling to keep encroaching whites at bay. The Utes and the Apaches, for instance, lived in areas where gold was discovered and also athwart the California trails to the goldfields there. Gold and silver prospectors rushing to California, the Rockies, and the Black Hills of the Dakotas had no respect for or patience with the Indians whose living spaces the miners destroyed. The U.S. government tried to hold back these miners—but not with much spirit. The U.S. Army found itself protecting miners, not Indians.

What happened to Chief Joseph's Nez Percé happened to the Indians again and again. They would resist, would fight, would flee, and often they would fend off the whites for a time. But in the end, they always lost: By the 1870s the U.S. Army had rapid-fire repeating rifles, the Hotchkiss gun, which fired exploding shells, as well as thousands of tough, experienced troops trained in the Civil War. Though Indians won many battles, U.S. troops won more, and in the end they won the wars.

Yet ironically, the most famous of all the Plains battles was an Indian victory. The leaders of the fight on both sides are still remembered—the great Indian chief Sitting Bull and the foolhardy General George Armstrong Custer.

As we have seen, the Sioux were the most powerful tribe on the Great Plains. They were, in fact, more than a tribe, really a loose-knit confederacy of bands who spoke the same language and followed many of the same folkways. Sitting Bull had become famous among them. At fourteen, in a battle against the Crows, he had charged nearly naked, his face painted yellow, into the enemy and knocked one of them from his horse with a tomahawk. He grew in stature, known not only for his fearlessness in battle but as a gentle man ready to spare the life of a captured foe and willing to share his supplies of buffalo meat and drink with friends. He came to be seen as a wise—indeed, a holy—man and rose to become a leader among the Sioux.

Implacably hostile to whites, Sitting Bull was not one to submit to life on a reservation planting corn. In 1868 the Sioux made a treaty with the

This picture of Sitting Bull shows great determination in his face. Representative of many Indians, he was ferocious in resisting assimilation into white culture.

U.S. government giving them, among other things, rights to their sacred Black Hills in what is today South Dakota. But in the winter of 1875–76, because gold had been discovered there, the government began pressing the Sioux to sell the Black Hills and go to a reservation.

Sitting Bull was not going to accept this. In the spring of 1876 he brought into his camp, in a river valley west of the Black Hills, a fighting force of between 2,500 and 4,000 men and boys. Meanwhile, the army was gathering its force, preparing to drive the Sioux and their allies off the Black Hills—an area that had been reserved for the Sioux by treaty. The soldiers advanced in three widely separated groups, hoping to catch the enemy in a pincers. Late in June the great warrior Crazy Horse encountered one of these groups, led by General George Crook, at Rosebud Creek in south-central Montana. They clashed viciously, and Crook backed off.

On June 22 George Armstrong Custer, leading another group, prepared to set off. A fellow officer said, "Now Custer, don't be greedy. Wait for us."

"No, I won't," Custer said. Did he mean he would not be greedy or would not wait? Events would tell. He left with about 600 men, looking

General George Armstrong Custer was just as determined a man as Sitting Bull. He had fought with distinction in the Civil War, and his death at the hands of the Indians enraged many white Americans.

for the Sioux village, which he thought to be somewhere in the valley of the Little Bighorn River, not too far from Rosebud Creek. Eventually his scouts spotted the village from a high point. Custer split his forces, sending one group of 125 to attack one end of the village, while he took 210 men around to the other end. The first group plunged toward the village, only to find it much larger than they had expected: Their little detachment was facing as many as 2,500 warriors. They halted and pulled back to a defensive position on a hilltop.

Now fully aroused, the Indians discovered Custer's group approaching from another direction. The Sioux charged out of their village at the band of confused soldiers. Caught in the open, the soldiers could only stand their ground and die. Within an hour Custer's little force lay dead on the Plains, General Custer among them.

The Battle of the Little Bighorn was the most celebrated of all Indian victories, but ironically, it was the beginning of the end for them. Custer had been a hero in the Civil War, much admired by northerners, and his death at the hands of the Indians angered many Americans. They demanded revenge. The U.S. government poured more troops into the fight. Very quickly the Sioux confederacy broke up. Thousands of Indians gave up and went onto reservations.

The Battle of the Little Bighorn is still one of the most famous in American history. Quite unimportant in a broad sense, it nonetheless had an inherent drama that captured people's imagination. Tens of thousands of pictures of Custer's Last Stand, many of them quite fanciful, hung on the walls of American homes, restaurants, saloons. This one shows Custer standing in the center, firing a pair of pistols.

But Sitting Bull would not quit. With a small band he went up into Canada. Bit by bit, however, his followers abandoned him, and in 1881 he surrendered with a remnant of 187 men, all that remained of the mighty force that had won the great victory at Little Bighorn. But still, as we shall see, Sitting Bull was not finished.

Nonetheless, by the 1880s the Indians of the Great Plains were feeling demoralized. Again and again they had been forced to move, forced to give up lands the U.S. government had agreed they should have. They saw no end to it. How would they keep their ancient culture alive?

They were in this mood when word began to spread among them of something that renewed their hope. In 1889 a Paiute Indian named Wovoka had a vision of a return to the time before the coming of the whites, when the buffalo had been plentiful. He began to preach, and quickly gathered followers.

Wovoka's teaching was nonviolent: The Indians should not make war against the whites, but should try to cooperate with them. In time the earth would shake, a new world would come, the dead would rise, people would be young, the buffalo would return. He taught the Indians a new Ghost Dance, which often brought on trancelike states. Wovoka's message fell on the ears of people hungry for hope, and people from other tribes came to hear him speak and join in the dance.

The new Ghost Dance religion worried whites. They feared that the dance was really a war dance—which it was not—and that a general uprising of the Indians was being planned. To halt it before it began, the Indian agents were told to stop the dancing, and the army prepared itself for war.

Most of the Indians obeyed Wovoka's command to remain at peace with the whites. But the Sioux had other ideas. They insisted that Ghost Dancers wore shirts that made them invisible and were impervious to soldiers' bullets. Sitting Bull was among those who decided to go along with the new religion sensing that the Ghost Dance cult might prove useful in the struggle against the whites. Sitting Bull became a leader in the new cult.

The army, knowing well Sitting Bull's reputation among the Sioux, decided to arrest him before he roused up the Indians. They knew that arresting him was risky, for the Indians might fight to protect him. They decided to go ahead anyway. Instead of sending soldiers, however, they sent in the members of the local constabulary made up of Indians. In December 1890, some forty-three men from the constabulary surrounded Sitting Bull's cabin. Three of them went inside, arrested Sitting Bull, and brought him out. At first Sitting Bull intended to go peacefully, but his supporters ran up to protect him. A scuffle broke out, a gun was fired, and two of the constabulary fired at Sitting Bull from close range and killed him. General fighting broke out, in which several Indians and constabulary were killed.

The death of Sitting Bull, however much it disheartened the Indians, did not end the Ghost Dance cult. The government decided to arrest another of the Ghost Dance leaders, Big Foot. Soldiers tracked him and a band of about 350 followers, mostly women and children, to encampment along a pleasant stream called Wounded Knee Creek.

Actually, Big Foot had lost confidence in the Ghost Dance religion. Moreover, he was sick, and when the soldiers surrounded his encampment he showed no signs of fighting. The soldiers mounted four of the recently developed Hotchkiss machine guns on a hill nearby, their muzzles aimed at the Indian tepees. Both groups settled in for the night. In the morning the soldiers began to search the Indian encampment for guns and powder. The Indians began to grow angry. One medicine man went among them urging them to fight: They could not be harmed because of their ghost shirts.

The soldiers became increasingly nervous. A gun was fired by accident, and quickly the soldiers fought their way out of the encampment. The Hotchkiss guns began to fire, slaughtering men, women, and children indiscriminately. In less than an hour it was over. At least 150 Indians were dead, along with twenty-five soldiers. The army later brought charges against the commander of the soldiers at Wounded Knee, but the charges were dismissed.

The Battle of Wounded Knee was by no means the worst slaughter perpetrated by both sides in the Indian wars, but it marked the end of Indian resistance against whites on the Great Plains, and it has symbolic meaning for many Indians today. In the end, the cult of the Ghost Dance was not a new beginning for the Indians, but the brief flare-up of a dying coal. Henceforward the whites would decide where and how Indians would live. The great warrior Red Cloud said, "I who used to control five

The body of Big Foot in the snow at Wounded Knee. The slaughter of Indians in this fight has not been forgotten and remains of great symbolic importance to American Indians.

thousand warriors, must tell Washington when I am hungry. I must beg for that which I own." Another Indian, Black Elk, was reported to have said, "The [Indian] nation's hoop was broken, and there was no center any longer for the flowering tree. The people were in despair. They seemed heavy to me, heavy and dark; so heavy that it seemed they could not be lifted; so dark that they could not be made to see any more."

The land that had been home to the Indians and the buffalo was no longer theirs. The nation, from sea to shining sea, belonged to the whites. Indians have not vanished from everywhere in the United States, of course. There are today many more Americans of full or part Indian descent than there were just two generations ago. But they no longer own the Great Plains.

CHAPTER III

The Legendary American Cowboy

No figure so typifies the American West as the cowboy. It is not the Indian, not the buffalo, not the gold miners we think of when we say "westerner," but the hard-bitten cowhand with his six-shooter, lariat, and faithful pony. Indeed, if you were to ask people elsewhere in the world who best symbolized America, many of them would instantly say the cowboy. Even today, when the trail-riding horseman has been gone for a century, we still use the word cowboy to mean somebody reckless and unfettered.

The cowboy came along with the cows—in this case the famous Texas longhorns. The Spanish had brought cattle to the Southwest long before; the longhorn was a mix of these cattle and other types brought in from England and the American East. Long legged, with horns spreading five feet wide, these cattle were "a butcher's nightmare," for they were stringy and yielded little meat for their size—"eight pounds of beef on 800 pounds of bone"—as the saying went. But they had two great advantages: They could survive the hard winters of the Plains, and with little good flesh to lose they lost little on the long trail drives to market. As early as the 1850s some Texans attempted to drive them east to market.

The Texas longhorn was considered a butcher's nightmare because the meat was tough and stringy, but millions of them were eaten by Americans. This beast has a horn spread of nine and a half feet.

The Civil War cut Texas off from the East, but with the end of the war the cattle boom began in earnest.

It was driven by two factors: the rapid decline of the buffalo, which opened the Plains to cattle, and the booming population of the cities of the East with their ever-increasing need for food. The population of the West, too, was rapidly increasing, especially in the California goldfields and the lush country of the Northwest. In addition, railroads extended their lines continually westward to meet the north-south cattle trails.

Furthermore, while some of the land of the Great Plains had been set aside for Indian reservations, and other parts remained under control of bellicose Indian tribes, most of it was in the "public domain"—that is, held by the federal government for the use of the American people. Ranchers let their herds roam over the prairies, sometimes having to bend the law by legal, though unethical, methods. The most common of these was to pay men to claim farmlands under the Homestead Act of

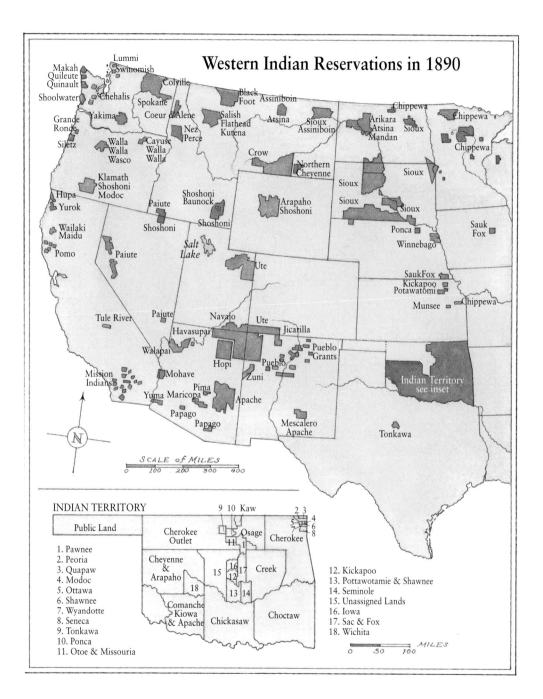

Western Indian Reservations in 1890

Lummi
Makah
Quileute
Quinault
Swinomish
Colville
Shoolwater
Chehalis
Black
Foot
Assiniboin
Chippewa
Spokane
Grande
Ronde
Yakima
Coeur d'Alene
Salish
Flathead
Kutena
Atsina
Sioux
Assiniboin
Arikara
Atsina
Mandan
Sioux
Chippewa
Nez
Perce
Siletz
Walla
Walla
Wasco
Cayuse
Walla
Walla
Crow
Chippewa
Klamath
Shoshoni
Modoc
Northern
Cheyenne
Sioux
Hupa
Yurok
Paiute
Shoshoni
Baunock
Arapaho
Shoshoni
Sioux
Sioux
Wailaki
Maidu
Shoshoni
Ponca
Sauk
Fox
Pomo
Paiute
Shoshoni
Salt
Lake
Winnebago
SaukFox
Kickapoo
Potawatomi
Ute
Tule River
Paiute
Navajo
Ute
Jicarilla
Munsee
Chippewa
Havasupai
Pueblo
Grants
Walapai
Hopi
Pueblo
Mission
Indians
Mohave
Zuni
Indian Territory
see inset
Yuma
Pima
Maricopa
Apache
Papago
Papago
Mescalero
Apache
Tonkawa

SCALE of MILES
0   100   200   300   400

N

INDIAN TERRITORY

| Public Land |

1. Pawnee
2. Peoria
3. Quapaw
4. Modoc
5. Ottawa
6. Shawnee
7. Wyandotte
8. Seneca
9. Tonkawa
10. Ponca
11. Otoe & Missouria

9 10 Kaw
2 3
4
5
6
7
8
Cherokee
Outlet
Osage
Cherokee
11   1
Cheyenne
&
Arapaho
15
16
17
12
Creek
18
13 14
Comanche
Kiowa
& Apache
Chickasaw
Choctaw

12. Kickapoo
13. Pottawotamie & Shawnee
14. Seminole
15. Unassigned Lands
16. Iowa
17. Sac & Fox
18. Wichita

MILES
0   50   100

1862, which permitted pioneer farmers to stake out 160 acres, and then let the cattle range over the land instead of cultivating it. In this way cattlemen began staking out claims to large portions of the Plains. Thus, under the Homestead Act, a man could put up a ranch house, often near a stream, and claim a large piece of land around it—usually with ill-defined borders.

Vast areas of the Plains were useless and valueless without a nearby water supply, so in effect the cattleman could let his herds range over huge tracts of land owned by the United States. Since the cattle of several ranchers roamed the same range, different brands were stamped on them with hot irons so owners could tell which were theirs. In the spring a great roundup took place, and calves identified as they ran by their mother's side were branded.

The biggest problem for these early cattlemen was getting the beasts to market, especially to the cities of the East a thousand or more miles away. Without modern refrigeration, the cattle had to be transported to places like Chicago to be butchered and the meat quickly distributed around the nation. The solution was to drive them across hundreds of wearying miles, through blazing heat and driving rain. The cowboys would round them up in the spring. Then they would set off with huge herds of cattle, sometimes thousands in a single drive.

But there were problems with the system. The Texas longhorns were infected with a tick that did not bother them but could cause serious illness to the domestic cattle of farmers farther east. These farmers insisted that the longhorns not be driven into their areas.

Fortunately for the cattlemen, just at this moment railroads were being pushed across the Plains, as we shall see in more detail shortly. At points along these railroad lines small towns, many hardly more than little villages, were springing up. In 1867 an investor named Joseph McCoy put a stockyard in one of these tiny towns, Abilene, Kansas. There was water nearby and good grazing land. Here McCoy built pens to hold cattle for shipment to the meat-processing plants in the cities of the East. If shipment was delayed, the cattle could be turned loose on the grazing land nearby. At first simply a collection of a dozen log huts with sod roofs, Abilene rapidly grew into a rough frontier town.

Very quickly similar shipping points at the end of the ever-westering railroad line

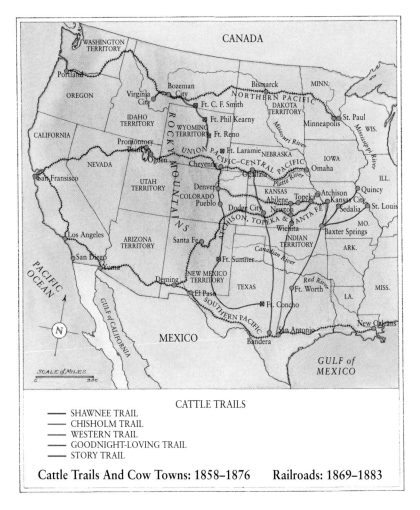

CATTLE TRAILS

—— SHAWNEE TRAIL
—— CHISHOLM TRAIL
—— WESTERN TRAIL
—— GOODNIGHT-LOVING TRAIL
—— STORY TRAIL

Cattle Trails And Cow Towns: 1858–1876   Railroads: 1869–1883

were set up in other towns, like Wichita and Dodge City. And it was around these towns that the legend of the gun-slinging cowboy grew up. The legend is, of course, much exaggerated. The reality of life for cowboys was mostly a great deal of very hard work for very little pay. Most of them carried small rifles—not the six-shooter of legend. The work involved long, often boring hours in the saddle, sometimes in driving blizzards, sometimes in dust and baking heat. The food was rough, and mostly they slept on the ground with rattlesnakes around. The work was dangerous: Rivers must be crossed, occasionally drowning cattle and cowboys together; cattle could stampede; there were wolves, snakes, Indians to contend with.

Inevitably, when these men came into a town like Abilene after months on the prairies, they wanted to spend their money having a good time. They drank in the saloons, gambled at poker tables. It is not surprising that at times fighting broke out. There was, in fact, far less violence in these cattle towns than movies and books would have us believe, but there was violence enough. In order to control it the cow towns brought in marshals and sheriffs to keep order, among them the celebrated Bat Masterson, Wild Bill Hickok, and Wyatt Earp. In fact, these lawmen, not the cowboys themselves, provided much of the stuff of the legendary West.

The famous cowtowns of movies and televisions were actually very rough places, with streets filled with mud that were barely traversable, and no sidewalks. This picture shows Deadwood, South Dakota, in 1876. Note the rough main street, and the shabby stores and shops. Such towns hardly amounted to a handful of blocks: The countryside began at the end of the main street.

For the cowboys, these forays into town were rare. Nonetheless, at least a part of the romance of the cowboy has some truth to it. Because the work was so hard, boring, and dangerous, and the pay so small, a great many newcomers quickly dropped out. Ranchers had constantly to recruit new young men from the East, many of them Civil War veterans from the South, which was slowly recovering from the devastation of the war.

More demanding than ranch work, was driving the cattle over hundreds of miles of rugged trail. If they stuck it out, the trail riders found themselves part of a clan of men who had a code of their own. A man had to be a good rider—there was no other choice. He had also to be courageous, willing to take the risks the job brought with it, like plunging into freezing rivers to rescue a horse, cow, or a fellow cowboy, standing up to bandits who stole cattle or to competing ranchers who branded their mavericks (a calf separated from its mother). These men took pride in their skills and endurance, and were deeply and mirthfully scornful of "tenderfeet" they met. Surrounded as they were by young men like themselves, fiercely independent and not inclined to back down from an affront, they learned to respect each other's feelings. A lot of cocky talk and boasting was not welcome. The sense of camaraderie was genuine. Overworked and underpaid, they nonetheless took a pride in themselves that men working in factories or clerking in stores might not feel.

The cowboy of film and book was white, but in fact as many as a third of them were black or Mexican. African-Americans in particular played a larger role in the history of the West than is generally recognized. After the Civil War, when former slaves, especially the men, were free to travel, thousands fled west to escape the new serfdom of the postwar South. They turned up in the mining camps, joined the army in the war against the Indians, and many of them became cowboys.

The West was not without racial prejudice—after all, a great many of the people streaming west had recently been slaveholders, or at least lived in a slave economy. Artists such as Frederic Remington and Theodore

Cowpunching could be dangerous work. This picture by Charles M. Russell shows a steer attacking a horse and his fallen rider, while another cowboy attempts to drag the steer away.

Davis depicted African-American soldiers on the frontier as "comic characters, especially when confronting face to face 'heap big Injuns,'" and chronicler of the Nebraska Plain Marie Sandoz described townsfolk as deeply resentful of the presence of black "protectors," and suggested that the Indians themselves might be better company. Nevertheless, there was wider acceptance of blacks on the Plains and in the mining camps than there was back east and in the South, where efforts were being made to return blacks to a serfdom that was not much different from the slavery so recently ended. (The plight of the freed slaves is described in the volume in this series called *Reconstruction and the Rise of Jim Crow.*)

The rise of what came to be called the "Cattle Kingdom" was very rapid. It began at the end of the Civil War in 1865, and by the late 1870s hundreds of thousands of branded cattle grazed the Plains. Besides the reduction of the buffalo herds and the collapse of Indian resistance, two innovations helped in this rapid rise. One was the invention of barbed wire in 1874. This was a type of wire with sharp points set along it every six inches or so, which could be strung rapidly across a prairie. Very quickly ranchers began to fence in their claims, sometimes including public land or the land of other ranchers. There were recriminations, fence cuttings, feuds, even gunfights, but the wire, in the main, stayed.

A second innovation was the introduction of deep-well drilling, with the wells pumped by wind. As the grass along riverbanks was cropped thin, cattle had to be pushed farther and farther away from water sources. The deep wells allowed ranchers to create ponds, pools, and watering troughs in the midst of empty prairies. With barbed wire and

Here Russell shows the other side of cowpunching—some cowboys riding into town with their pay, looking for some fun.

Charlie Russell, as everyone called him, admitted that he was never more than a fair cowboy himself, but his many years in the West allowed him to picture cowboy life with an accuracy missing from the work of many others.

deep wells, the open range style of ranching diminished; ranchers now worked enclosed pastures and watered their cattle from these "tanks."

Once it became clear that a great deal of money could be made in cattle, investors jumped in, many of them Europeans, particularly the English, Scots, and Germans. If a person could get even a small amount of financing and put together a herd of cattle, he could find a place to graze them. The number of cattle on the Plains swelled fearsomely: By the 1880s there were an estimated 7.5 million head of cattle on the Plains north of Texas. Inevitably, the land was overgrazed, especially in the southern Plains, where it all began: In 1870 it took five acres of land to support one cow; ten years later it took fifty acres. Ranchers also began to move their herds northward to meet the railroad lines. At the same time they started introducing cattle from elsewhere, especially white-faced Herefords, which reached maturity faster and carried more meat than did the longhorns. The longhorns, in addition, were still carrying ticks and Texas fever: Many states began trying to keep the longhorns out. New types of tick-free cattle, sometimes crossbred with longhorns, began to take over.

The booming cattle industry had occasional ups and downs, due to bad weather, overproduction, and other causes, but mostly the trend was up through the 1870s and into the 1880s. The boom reached a peak in 1882, when range cattle were selling for $30 to $35 each, and profits were huge. As is typical in booms of this kind, people began to lose sight of reality. Everybody who could raise any money was pushing cattle onto the land. With an oversupply of beef, prices began to go down: By 1884 the price per head was $8 or $10, a third of what it had been two years earlier.

But worse was to come. The winter of 1885–86 in the southern Plains was one of the worst ever to hit that area. During blinding snowstorms cattle drifted into the barbed wire fences where they were trapped, and died by the tens of thousands. Some ranchers claimed to have lost 85 percent of their herds, although most did not suffer such extreme losses.

The following summer there was a drought across the northern Plains, where the Cattle Kingdom was now focused. The grass was sparse, and cattle crowding around streams and water holes trampled down what grass remained in these areas. Then that winter, 1886–87, there came blizzards like none that anyone could remember. Temperatures dropped to as low as 46 degrees below zero, so that the cowboys had to huddle by their stoves for days at an end, rather than tend to the cattle. All winter driving snow and fearful temperatures slashed at the cattle. It was, one rancher said, "Hell without heat." Cowboys trying to save the cattle in the deep snow could hardly save themselves. "The horse's feet were cut and bleeding from the heavy crust, and the cattle had the hair and hide worn off their legs to the knees and hocks." When spring came ranchers found the lands littered with rotting cattle, and in the swollen streams dead cattle were rolling over and over. President-to-be Theodore Roosevelt, who loved the West, was utterly discouraged when he visited his own ranch that spring. He said, "In its present form, stock-raising on the plains is doomed and can hardly outlast the century . . . We who have felt the charm of life, and have exulted in its abounding vigor and its bold, restless freedom . . . must also feel real sorrow that those who come after us are not to see, as we have seen, what is perhaps the pleasantest, healthiest, and most exciting phase of American existence."

Roosevelt was surely romanticizing the hard life of the cowboys, and the pain the loss of the buffalo had brought to the Indians, but he was right in saying that the day of the old-fashioned cowboy was gone.

The heyday of the Cattle Kingdom was a brief twenty years. Its death was caused by many factors, but the coming of barbed wire, which allowed cattle to be more easier controlled, was one of them. This picture by yet another famous Western artist, Frederic S. Remington, called The Fall of the Cowboy, *shows that by the 1890s, cowpunching had become routine work.*

The Six-Shooter

The Colt six-shooter is almost as much a legend as the westerners who carried it, and justly so, for it had important consequences for the American conquest of the Great Plains. Before its invention, guns of any kind could only fire one shot without reloading, a process that took about a minute. An Indian could shoot several arrows from a bow in a minute. They learned to wait until enemy troops had fired their guns and then swoop in to fire several arrows at close range. Indians could usually fight off soldiers unless vastly outnumbered. In the woodlands of the East, where people were mostly afoot, the weapon of choice for hunting was the long rifle, which, however slow, was very accurate.

In the West, however, a man on horseback could not easily aim a rifle even when the horse was standing still; slight movements of the horse would throw the aim off.

In 1830 a sixteen-year-old boy named Samuel Colt devised a pistol that could fire six shots without reloading. (There was also a five-shot pistol, but the six-shooter is best known.) The Colt pistol was equipped with a cylinder for holding six bullets. The force of each shot revolved the cylinder to bring a new bullet into place behind the barrel. Eventually Colt got backers, built a factory in Paterson, New Jersey, and began to turn out the Colt six-shooters.

However, Colt could not interest the U.S. Army in buying the new weapon. But some of the guns happened to come to the attention of the famous Texas Rangers, whose main job was to fight Indians. The Rangers took to the Colt immediately. In a fight at Pedernales a fifteen-man unit of Rangers was attacked by about seventy Comanches. With their revolving pistols the Rangers quickly killed thirty of the Indians and the rest fled. The Colt six-shooter had proved itself.

But because the U.S. Army had not taken up the weapon, sales had been small, and poor Sam Colt had gone bankrupt. Then, during the Mexican War in 1846, army officers observed the effectiveness of the six-shooter in the hands of the Texas Rangers. The army placed a big order, and in a few years Samuel Colt, by that time relocated to Hartford, Connecticut, was a millionaire. And by the time of the rise of the Cattle Kingdom, the Colt six-shooter was known throughout the West. It may not have become as much a part of a cowboy's equipment as his boots or his broad-brimmed hat, but many carried one, and the famous Texas Rangers made the six-shooter their standard sidearm.

Ranchers went bankrupt, investors pulled out; most of the usable open land was now fenced off, or being settled by sheep and wheat farmers. Cowboys still spent many hours in the saddle, but now they were as likely to sleep in bunkhouses as on bedrolls on the prairie, eat their dinners in a ranch mess hall instead of around a campfire. Cattle ranching was becoming a business like any other.

From beginning to end the Cattle Kingdom and the cowboy life of our romantic fiction had lasted a mere twenty years. But its effect on the mythology of America has been profound. None of the other great epics of American history—like the suffering of the Mayflower Pilgrims, the battle to create our great Constitution, the tragic story of the Civil War—has played so large a role in the American mind as has the tale of the cowboy of the Great Plains. There are cowboys in the American West today—thousands of them; but few ride horses and fewer still carry revolving six-shooters.

CHAPTER IV

The Railroads Go West

As should be clear at this point, the conquest of the Great Plains could not have occurred without the railroad. Without the railroad to carry mountains of hides east, the depletion of the buffalo would not have come about so swiftly. Without the railroad to ship cattle east, the Cattle Kingdom would not have developed as it did. And as we shall see shortly, without the railroad to carry vast tons of wheat and other crops east, farmers could not have taken over the Plains as they ultimately did.

Originally, transportation in the new, undeveloped United States had been mainly by water—up and down the coasts, through rivers and lakes, and eventually through canals connecting natural bodies of water, like the famous Erie Canal, which tied the Great Lakes and the Mississippi River system to the Atlantic ports and foreign lands beyond them. By the 1830s railroad lines were developing. These grew haphazardly and unsystematically, accompanied by a great deal of chicanery. The rapidly growing towns and cities of the East felt that they must be on a railroad line for the sake of their businesses. So eager for rail service were many of these town fathers that they gave to the railroads land for lines and

The Ohio River was a major part of the great inland water chain that constituted the main transportation system of America before the coming of the railroads. Cities like Cincinnati, shown here in the 1830s, flourished along this water system.

stations, lent them vast sums of money, freed them from taxes, and helped in other ways. The railroads paid huge sums in bribes, often produced shoddy systems, and in some cases never built the lines they had been paid for. The construction of the American railroads, especially after the Civil War, is one of the great scandals in American history. But eventually the many lines were pulled together into a great transportation system without which the development of the Great Plains would not have been nearly so rapid as it was. (The story of the transportation revolution is told in the volume in this series called *Andrew Jackson's America.*)

Like the East, in the West transportation was originally by water. The first American settlers to the West Coast came by ship, mainly the fast clipper ships of the 1850s that were making the United States a powerful maritime force. But where the East, even before the canals were dug, had a complex system of natural waterways, including the Ohio and Mississippi River system, the Great Lakes and St. Lawrence system, other

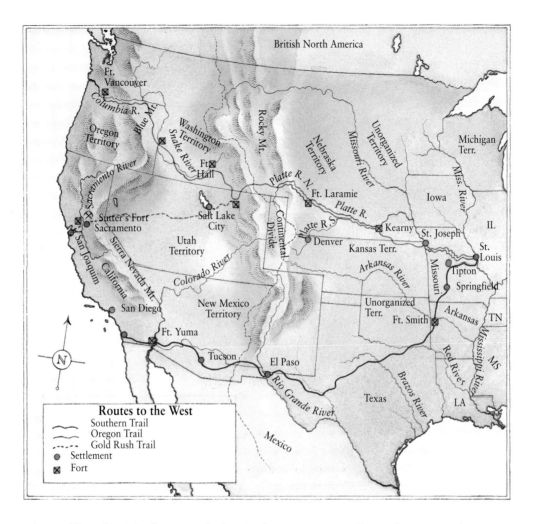

Routes to the West
- ～ Southern Trail
- ～ Oregon Trail
- ---- Gold Rush Trail
- ● Settlement
- ⊠ Fort

rivers like the Hudson and the Delaware, as well as the coastal water-ways of the Atlantic and Gulf of Mexico, the West had few year-round navigable rivers: The Missouri and its branches provided some access to the northern part of the Great Plains, and a few other rivers, like the Arkansas, the Platte, and the Red, ran out of the Rockies into the Mississippi. But unlike the East, where there was always some sort of stream leading into a larger network of rivers within a few miles of most householders, in the West navigable rivers and streams might lie a hundred miles apart. Further, in dry seasons many of these rivers could become too shallow for large boats.

After the Mexican War and the start of the gold rush, it became clear that the West could not grow without an overland transportation system. One of the earliest was the famous stagecoach, which has appeared in almost every western movie made. The stagecoach business was started in 1857 when the U.S. government backed a promoter named John Butterfield to build a system to carry the mails between California and Missouri, from where there were already rail lines to the East. Eventually Butterfield had stagecoaches connecting St. Louis, Santa Fe, Denver, Virginia City, and San Francisco. They ran twice a week and made the journey from San Francisco to St. Louis in twenty-two days. Other stage-coach concerns were started to carry passengers and some freight as well as the mail. Twenty-two days was a long time to wait for a letter, but it was considerably shorter than the time it took for sailing ships from the

There were far fewer rivers in the West than there were in the East. At first the famous stagecoaches, like this Concord Stage, supplied much of the passenger, mail, and freight transportation.

Pacific Coast going around the bottom of South America to get to the cities of the Atlantic Coast.

In order to provide speedier mail service, the famous Pony Express was set up. In this system, 115 way stations were established between California and St. Joseph, Missouri. A rider would charge out of his station and gallop his horse for ten miles without pause. At the next way station he would fling the mailbag to a waiting rider, who would charge over to the succeeding station. The trip across almost 2,000 miles was made in ten days. Speed was everything: The riders were small and wiry and carried the minimum of equipment to save weight. The price for a one ounce letter was ten dollars, a lot of money for the time. The romantic Pony Express lasted only for two years—1860–61—when the telegraph rolled across the prairie and killed it.

But despite the partial successes of the stagecoach lines and the Pony Express, it was clear that the Plains West could not develop without railroads. The idea of building a transcontinental railroad line was obvious, and had come up even before the gold rush brought all those Americans flooding out to the Pacific Coast. It was equally obvious that building such a line was going to be terribly expensive. That by itself might not have been a problem, but nobody could see how any money could be

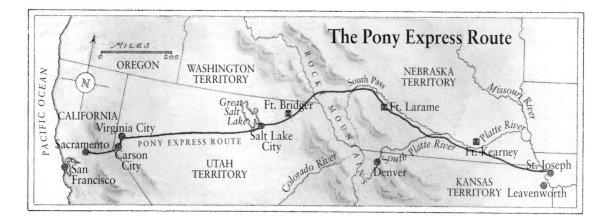

made from such a line. In the East railroads tied populous towns and cities together and connected them as well to farmlands producing all sorts of items needed in huge amounts by city dwellers. Despite an "orgy of railroad construction," there was plenty of business for railroads in the East. In the West, by contrast, there was only one small city, San Francisco, which in 1850 had a population of 50,000. On the vast prairies there were no cities at all, and only a few small towns. There would hardly be enough business to support one rail line, much less many. (The development of the railroads before the Civil War is described in the volume in this series called *The Rise of Industry*.)

However, the U.S. government had good reasons for wanting a railroad line built. For one thing, until 1846 the British and Mexicans had interests on the Pacific Coast they wanted to protect. The U.S. government wanted to be able to move troops and equipment rapidly to the West Coast to counter threats by other nations. For another thing, it was generally believed that it would be much to the nation's advantage to displace the Indians and occupy both the Great Plains and the regions west of the Rocky Mountains to make sure they were firmly American. Among other things, huge numbers of immigrants flooding in were filling eastern cities to bursting; more room was needed.

The government thus decided that it had to promote a railroad line across the Plains. In 1853 Congress allocated money for surveys, and army engineers went west. They found seven possible routes for rail lines, four of which seemed most practical. Two of these crossed the southern part of the trans-Mississippi west, two the northern part (trans means across, on the other side). It was felt that the nation could only afford to build on one of these routes. The North and the South were already growing increasingly hostile to each other in the struggle that would in a few years lead to the Civil War, and neither wanted the other to have control over a transcontinental line running through its territory. So nothing could be done.

But with the outbreak of the Civil War the federal government fell into the hands of the North, and in 1862 a northerly route was chosen to run from Sacramento, California, to the Missouri River. The railroads, of course, would be built and run by private companies, not the government. The Union Pacific Railroad Company would build from the Missouri River westward, the Central Pacific would build from Sacramento eastward. Much of the necessary capital would come from investors who bought stock; the rest of the money would come from the government in the form of loans, running to tens of millions of dollars. In addition, the railroads were given huge amounts of land along the right of way to do with as they pleased.

This arrangement, especially the land grants, was, and still is, highly controversial. Land at any distance from the railroad would remain relatively worthless, while land along the line might become exceedingly valuable. The railroads, by controlling roughly half of the land along their own lines, would be in a position to sell that land—that without the railroad would be worth little—at very high prices. They could, and did, lay out towns along the lines, and as the towns grew the railroads sold their holdings at enormous profits. There would have been no profits without the railroads, of course, but neither would there have been the towns.

Some historians today say that the railroads did not profit unduly from this arrangement: Most of the loans were paid back, and the railroads eventually saved the government millions by carrying the mails at cheap rates. But there is no getting around the fact that a lot of bribes were paid, although mostly to state and local, rather than federal, officials. It is also true that railroad promoters enriched themselves at the expense of stockholders and the public generally through various dubious schemes. The most widespread of these was for railroad chiefs to set up separate construction companies, which they owned, to lay the rail lines. As managers of the construction companies they would overcharge themselves as managers of the railroad companies, and pay themselves no matter how high the price was. The railroad stockholders would get nothing, while the owners of the construction companies would collect hugely inflated profits. Graft and corruption with government help made a few railroad developers enormously wealthy. But at the same time farms and other real estate on the Great Plains wouldn't have been worth much or been profitable at all without the railroads.

The question is, Why didn't the government simply have the Army Corps of Engineers build the line, which it was capable of doing? After all, in virtually every other nation in the world, the government built and ran the railroads. This makes a certain amount of sense because the profit motive does not work if no one lives along the planned railroad route as was the case on much of the Great Plains. The private railroad companies had to find a profit somewhere, and in the early years they found it by selling land. Given the exorbitant profits and the bribes, government ownership would certainly have saved the taxpayers a great deal of money.

The answer is partly that too many people in local, state, and federal governments had something to gain from letting private companies build the railroads. But more significantly the American system has always been to keep governments from competing with private industry. Private enterprise in most industries has brought consumers, workers, and stockholders great benefits. Of course it is also true that private industry is not shy about asking for government aid when in trouble. Eventually, in the twentieth century, the government had to take over many railroads at the taxpayers' expense to keep them operating.

Work on the Union Pacific and Central Pacific lines began in 1863, but only after the Civil War ended was a concerted push made to complete them. Most of the hard work was done by immigrants—Irish immigrants coming from the east; Chinese laborers coming from the west. The Irish had it relatively easy, for most of the track was laid over the flat plains. The Chinese, however, had to cut through hundreds of miles of mountain

Chinese laborers, like these shown here, did much of the hard work to build the western end of the intercontinental rail-road line, chipping away at mountain-sides by hand to cut the rail bed.

ranges, boring tunnels through solid rock, cutting track bases out of mountain ranges, running bridges across gorges. This was in a day before power drills and massive earth movers: The Chinese pain-fully chipped away at the rock with hand tools, sometimes averaging only eight inches of track laid a day. But they pushed on.

As the two competing lines coming from east and west approached each other, it was clear that they would not meet, but were going to run past each other despite the fact that sometimes blasting from one line was so close to the other that workers were jarred by it. Finally the government insisted that the lines link up at a place called Promontory Summit, west of Ogden, Utah. On May 8, 1869, the rails were ready to be con-

This famous painting, called The Last Spike, *shows the head of the Union Pacific, Leland Stanford, about to drive the final spike that would complete the track. Actually, according to the artist, Stanford had ordered him to put into the painting friends of Stanford who were not there. The photograph, on the other hand, shows the scene as it was.*

nected, and two days later a throng of workers, dignitaries, officials, and reporters gathered. Leland Stanford, head of the Central Pacific, was given the honor of driving the last spike. All around America people were waiting to hear by telegraph that the great railroad line was completed. Stanford stood over the final spike, and swung his sledgehammer. Clang! Finally the nation was linked by rail from coast to coast. Pioneers making the trip trudging beside their covered wagons across the Plains and over the mountains from the Mississippi to the Pacific Coast struggled for three or four months in 1865. Four years later they could cover the same ground in ten days—sitting down on cushioned seats.

CHAPTER V

Settling the Plains

With the driving of the last spike at Promontory Summit it was clear that railroads could be built across the prairies, and that lots of money could be made from building them. Promoters rushed in and other lines were driven across the northern and southern ends of the Plains. From these, branch lines were built, eventually drawing western railroads into a system as had been done in the East.

To most Americans the building of these transcontinental lines was little short of a miracle. Where only a few years before the overlanders had labored for weeks to cross to California, now the trip could be made in comfort in days. To the Indians, however, the railroads were a disaster. The noisy, smoky trains roaring through what had once been quiet plains disrupted life for everything and everybody—plants, animals, humans. Railroad lines were normally laid where the terrain was suitable, and that sometimes was across land that had been reserved to the Indians by treaty. The railroads, as we have seen, had been granted huge amounts of land along the lines, and when the lines ran through Indian territory, so did the land grants. The government then set about revising its Indian treaties in order to force the Indians off the railroad lands. For

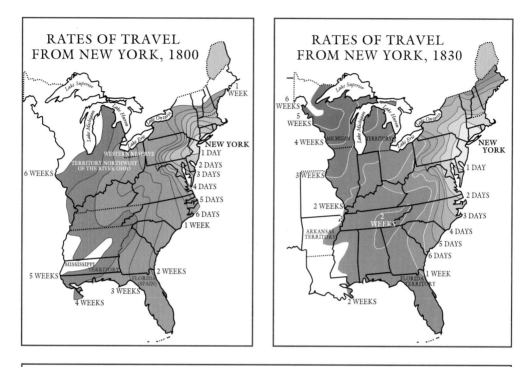

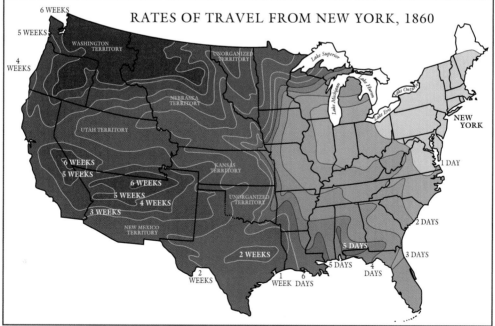

yet another thing, the railroads made it far easier for white buffalo hunters to reach their quarry, easier to transport mountains of buffalo hides. In fact, passengers sometimes shot their prey directly from railroad cars just for sport.

From the Indians' view point, there was nothing good about the railroads. Mounted warriors sometimes attacked construction crews and pulled up sections of track. Soldiers were posted to guard the crews, and sometimes retaliated by raiding Indian villages. The railroads, thus, intensified the antagonisms of the Indian and white conflict already under way.

But the worst of the problems brought to the Plains Indians by the railroads was simply that the lines opened the Indians' land for settlement by homesteaders, cattlemen, sheepherders. Throughout the first three hundred years after the first Englishmen arrived in America, land was the great preoccupation of the people. Wealth came from the land in the form of timber, wheat, salt pork, cotton, anything that grew. A person with nothing but land could, with luck and hard work, make money, indeed in some cases grow wealthy.

For three hundred years it had always seemed to Americans that there was plenty of land out there for the taking—first the land along the Atlantic Coast, then the land over the Alleghenies, and later on the Pacific coast; and finally the Great Plains. As we have seen, the fact that the Indians who lived there also claimed the land did not much concern the white settlers, although there were always some who were troubled by the Indians' fate. It seemed to most whites that the Indians were not making good use of the land, while the whites would. (After many generations of living on the Plains, Indian populations seldom reached densities of two people per square mile. After a single generation of settlement by pioneer farmers densities reached twelve and even more people per square mile.)

The problem, then, was how to see that this vast treasury of land was fairly distributed among the new settlers. It was generally agreed that the

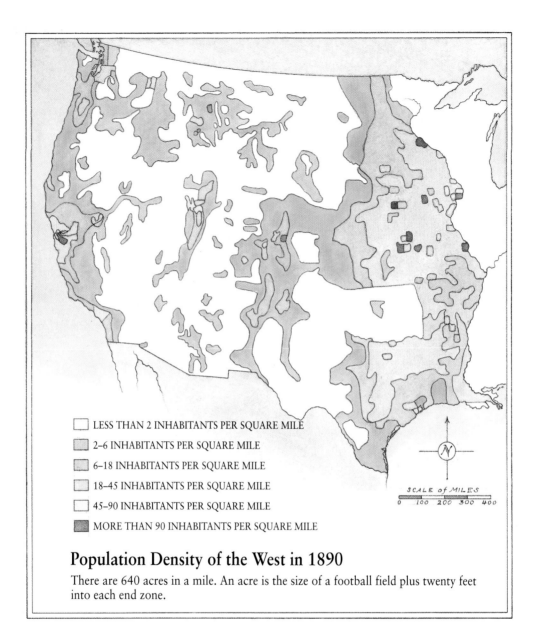

LESS THAN 2 INHABITANTS PER SQUARE MILE

2–6 INHABITANTS PER SQUARE MILE

6–18 INHABITANTS PER SQUARE MILE

18–45 INHABITANTS PER SQUARE MILE

45–90 INHABITANTS PER SQUARE MILE

MORE THAN 90 INHABITANTS PER SQUARE MILE

SCALE of MILES
0   100   200   300   400

Population Density of the West in 1890

There are 640 acres in a mile. An acre is the size of a football field plus twenty feet into each end zone.

strength of the nation lay in its "yeoman" farmers, the independent farm families relatively self-sufficient on their own land, who constituted the majority of Americans before the twentieth century: Not for America the system that existed in Europe, where a mass of peasants toiled on the land owned by a handful of wealthy landlords. The point was to make

Land along railroad lines was far more valuable than land at some distance. Very quickly villages grew up along the rail lines; some turned into towns, and then cities. Soon the empty prairie around the towns was plowed, at great labor, into farms.

sure that the land was evenly distributed among people who would farm it, rather than let it fall into the hands of a few large landholders, as sometimes happened.

Furthermore, Americans believed that their country could not become a great nation until the wilderness was tamed, and the land filled with people. They encouraged immigration, and this meant that the immigrants had to be able to get land for their own farms.

Various schemes for land distribution were worked out, the principal one being the Homestead Act of 1862. This act granted, for the payment of a small fee, a "quarter" of a square mile, or 160 acres, to anybody who could start a farm and keep it going for five years. (A standard football field including one end zone is just about one acre.) Over time millions of Americans took up these homestead grants. Many failed for one reason or another, but the majority prospered, and the white population spread westward at a rapid pace, driving the Indians before it.

However, as is often the case, the system did not work out in practice nearly as well as it was intended to. Despite all precautions, a lot of the land fell into the hands of speculators—people who had no intention of homesteading the land, but wanted merely to buy up as much as they could, to sell at a profit to other speculators or to people who actually intended to farm it. Part of the problem lay in the fact that it was easier for the government to sell off the land in large chunks; and only people with money could afford to buy large pieces, which they did in order to speculate. Homesteaders often had to buy their parcels from these speculators, paying more than they ought to have, and often burdening themselves with heavy mortgages. The biggest of these mortgage holders were the railroads.

Part of the problem lay in the fact that the old quarter sections, large enough for self-sufficient farms in the rain-rich lands east of the Mississippi, were not big enough for farms on the Plains. Stockherders needed far more than 160 acres for even a small herd of cattle or sheep; and farmers growing wheat, which became the primary, although not the only, crop of the Great Plains, also needed more acres.

But the main problem was that as much as the United States government wanted to encourage self-sufficient farmers on the Plains, it also bent to the wishes of ambitious men. As has usually been the case with governments everywhere, people with money and power were able to influence officeholders to favor their schemes. As we have seen, immense amounts of land were given to railroad corporations to do with as they wished for their own profit. Inevitably, these corporations tended to hang onto the land, waiting for the price to rise. Other huge amounts of land were given to the new states carved out of the Plains to sell to raise money for various purposes. Inevitably, speculators got hold of large

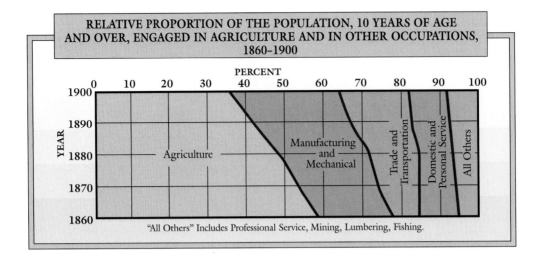

RELATIVE PROPORTION OF THE POPULATION, 10 YEARS OF AGE AND OVER, ENGAGED IN AGRICULTURE AND IN OTHER OCCUPATIONS, 1860–1900

PERCENT

"All Others" Includes Professional Service, Mining, Lumbering, Fishing.

AGRICULTURE S SHARE OF NATIONAL WEALTH, BY DECADES, 1860—1900

(VALUES IN BILLIONS)

CENSUS YEAR	NATIONAL WEALTH	AGRICULTURAL WEALTH	
			PERCENT OF NATIONAL
1900	$126.7	$20.4	16.1
1890	78.5	16.1	20.5
1880	49.9	12.2	24.4
1870	30.4	8.9	29.3

AGRICULTURAL WEALTH, BY SECTIONS AND DECADES, 1860—1900

(VALUES IN BILLIONS)

AREA	1860	1870	1880	1890	1900
United States	$7.980	$8.945	$12.181	$16.082	$20.440
North Atlantic	2.454	2.947	3.197	2.970	2.951
South Atlantic	1.207	.741	1.053	1.333	1.454
North Central	2.523	4.109	6.108	8.518	11.505
South Central	1.672	.907	1.290	1.891	2.816
Western	.123	.241	.532	1.371	1.715

These charts show that agricultural production in the United States increased by about 2 ½ times between 1860 and 1890, with virtually the entire increase coming from the Great Plains. At the same time, industrial production increased so much more that agriculture's share of the nation's wealth fell from about 40 percent to about 16 percent, and the percent of the total workforce engaged in agriculture fell from about 60 percent to about 35 percent. Today it is less than 2 percent.

POPULATION GROWTH OF THE GREAT PLAINS STATES 1870–1900		
	1870	**1900**
Arizona	10,000	123,000
Colorado	40,000	540,000
Idaho	15,000	165,000
Kansas	369,000	1,470,000
Montana	21,000	243,000
Nebraska	123,000	1,066,000
Nevada	42,000	42,000
New Mexico	92,000	195,000
North Dakota	2,000	319,000
Oklahoma	259,000 (1890)	790,000
South Dakota	12,000	402,000
Texas	819,000	3,049,000
Utah	87,000	277,000

HOURS AND WAGES BY HAND AND BY MACHINE

Comparison of hours of human labor and wages for the production of one acre each of different crops by hand methods (mainly) and by machine methods.

	TIME WORKED				LABOR COST	
	Hand		**Machine**			
	hours	minutes	hours	minutes		
Wheat	61	5	3	19	$ 3.56	$ .66
Corn	38	45	15	8	3.63	1.51
Oats	66	15	7	6	3.73	1.07
Hay: loose	21	5	3	57	1.75	.42
Hay: baled	35	30	11	34	3.06	1.29
Potatoes	108	55	38	0	10.89	3.80
Cotton	167	48	78	42	7.88	7.87
Rice: rough	62	5	17	3	5.64	1.01
Sugar cane	351	21	191	33	31.94	11.32
Tobacco	311	23	252	55	23.35	25.12
TOTAL: 10 crops	1,194	12	619	15	95.43	54.07
TOTAL: 27 different crops	9,760	48	5,107	53	$1,037.76	$598.13

chunks of the Plains, often through the payment of bribes and other favors to local, state, and federal officials, but more often just by bending the law a bit with the help of government agents who thought they were patriotically helping the nation grow.

Yet the promise of land was great and the people came. Some of them uprooted themselves from the East: from New England, where the soil was growing thin; and from New York, Pennsylvania, and Virginia, where overcrowding made land prices high; from everywhere where there no longer were farms for everybody. Many came from places like Indiana and Illinois, lured by the prospect of new land. After the Civil War people came out from the impoverished South, a lot of them to Texas. Among them were many African-Americans, trying to escape the sharecropping system there that was pushing them back into serfdom.

Huge numbers came from abroad, especially Germany and the Scandinavian countries. Immigrants tended to move into American cities to work in factories, but millions took up farming, a life many of them had known at home. By 1900 almost a third of the people in Texas were German-born and their children and grandchildren. Large numbers of Swedes and Norwegians took up homesteads on the prairies. By the 1880s there were farm settlements of Irish in Nebraska, Kansas, and Arkansas. Still, the largest number of those flooding onto the Plains were transplanted Americans, hoping to better their lives. (The story of these immigrants is told in the volume in this series called *A Century of Immigration*.)

They quickly found that it was easier said than done. For one thing, the tightly matted soil, with its deep root system that had been developing for hundreds of years, was terribly difficult to cut through. The old wooden and cast-iron plows of the East in most cases would not do. Just "breaking" the land was in itself a physically exhausting chore.

Then there were intermittent droughts. Some years there was simply not enough rain: Wheat withered in the fields and died, leaving the land

A typical sod house. Practically windowless, it would have been very gloomy inside. The landscape around is almost without features, and the farm family looks correspondingly gloomy. Nonetheless, many of these families prospered, despite everything.

brown. From time to time plagues of locusts and other insects swept like a great cloud miles long through the fields with a roaring sound, eating the crops while the farmers stood helplessly by and watched their livelihoods disappear in a morning. By the 1870s some farmers had windmills to draw water from deep under ground during dry spells, and steel sod-breaking plows; but many homesteaders could not afford these improvements.

The work was terribly hard and not always rewarding, but living conditions were equally bad. The treeless plain did not offer the wood that settlers in the East had readily available for houses and barns, and fireplaces and stoves. Many of the Plains farmers started off in sod houses. They would cut the thick turf into pieces a foot wide and three feet long. These would be dragged into place and stacked up about seven feet high to make a shelter perhaps eighteen by twenty-four feet, about the size of a good-sized modern living room. A few log rafters were set in place, and covered over with more sod. The sod would knit together: Wildflowers might grow in the roof. Such a building was strong enough to withstand the terrible winds that often sliced across the prairies, were relatively cool in the summer, and provided some insulation in the winter. But dirt fell from the roof; only a small amount of light came in through the door and one or two windows. The room was smoky and crowded.

If the family prospered through luck and endless hard work, they would in time be able to buy lumber and glass for a real house, turning the sod house into a shelter for animals. But there always remained the bleakness of the prairie, the view unbroken for miles by the hills, mountains, and streams the farm people had known back East or across the seas in Bavaria. Nor was there much company; farm families often lived miles apart, and in any case had little leisure for visiting.

It was the wives who seemed to have suffered the most. Hamlin Garland, a well-known writer of the nineteenth century who spent part of his youth on the prairie, summed it up in his poem, "The Farmer's Wife":

> *"Born an' scrubbed, suffered and died."*
> *That's all you need to say, elder.*
> *Never mind sayin' "made a bride,"*
> *Nor when her hair got gray.*
> *Jes' say, "born'n worked t' death":*
> *That fits it—save y'r breath.*

Wives and mothers, and in time their daughters, played—as always in family-run agriculture—a central role. Many families depended on the women's kitchen gardens for their food during the first year or two of pioneer farming while the men worked to establish the cultivated acres where a cash crop of wheat or corn would grow. Women, too, kept chickens and milk cows and brought in much-needed cash by selling eggs and butter.

Thus despite everything, many of these desperately overworked farm families managed somehow to prosper. They even created active social lives for themselves when they could, with dances, horse racing, and musicales. And after awhile small towns dotted the prairie, places for stores, churches, schools, theaters, and other spots for lonely farm families to gather at for social as well as economic activities.

Perhaps the main reason why the Plains farmers finally succeeded, besides the hard work they put in, were the extraordinary technological advances in farm machinery that came during the second half of the nineteenth century. It was a time of enormous inventiveness in any case, a period that saw the development of the telegraph, telephone, sound recorder, automobile, electric light and electric motor, the airplane and much else. Even though millions of Americans were leaving farms to go to work in city factories, agriculture was still the nation's largest business. A new improved plow or hay rake could sell in the tens of thousands, even hundreds of thousands, and make fortunes for the inventors. As a result inventors everywhere, many of whom had grown up on farms themselves and knew about farm work, were trying to devise better farm equipment.

By 1899 the U.S. Patent Office had issued over 9,000 patents for improvements to seeders and planters, and over 12,000 for plows. The inventions tumbled out one after another. Plows were doubled and doubled again to cut up to sixteen furrows at once. Great "combines" were developed that would not only reap (cut) the wheat but thresh it (separate the seeds from the stalks) and then tie the sheaves (stalks) into bundles. Some of the new reapers cut a swath across a field fifty feet wide. A vast array of improved hay rakes, bailers, cream separators, reapers, and churns came onto the market. The hours needed to do farm jobs plummeted. Where it had taken sixty-one hours to produce an acre of wheat by hand in 1830, in 1890 the job could be done by machines in three hours. For hay the time dropped from thirty-five hours to twelve hours—and other crops told the same story.

The existence of all this advanced farm machinery made possible what were called bonanza farms—bonanza was the word miners used for a particularly rich pocket of gold or silver ore. These vast farms were tens of thousands of acres. One, the Dalrymple holding, was *one hundred thousand* acres—156 square miles, a hundred thousand football fields—a piece of land as big as some eastern counties. Some of these great bonanza farms were worked by hundreds of men, mostly migrant laborers who went to where the work was as the seasons shifted, sometimes working thirteen-hour days for perhaps $10 a week, plus room and board.

But these bonanza farms were a minority, producing in total only a small percentage of the wheat and other crops that came out of the West. Most of the produce came from the small family farms. The fact that any of these farmers prospered, faced as they were by drought, hail, locusts, and blizzards, was a miracle; but they did. In the end, however, it turned out—at least from their limited perspective—that their worst enemies were human.

Although America was rapidly becoming industrialized, until the end of the nineteenth century, agriculture was the nation's first business. Inventors of agricultural equipment had a ready market. This advertisement for a planting "drill" promised savings in the millions.

CHAPTER VI

The Farmers Fight Back

The 1870s and 1880s saw the United States undergoing rapid and dramatic change. For one thing, a new massive immigration, beginning in the 1870s, combined with the innovations and inventions of the post–Civil War period, were turning the nation into one of cities and factories, rather than of villages and farms. Railroads were replacing canal barges and stagecoaches. People were buying their clothes, soap, bread, and many other items from shops, department stores, and mail-order catalogs, instead of making them at home. Most significantly from the farmers' viewpoint, control of production was no longer spread widely across thousands of small mills and shops and millions of farms but was increasingly falling to the hands of a relatively small number of people who held power in large corporations. Through the post–Civil War period this movement intensified, as smaller companies combined to form corporate giants like U.S. Steel, the Pennsylvania Railroad, the great banking complex headed by J. P. Morgan, itself so powerful that it once had to bail the U.S. government out of economic difficulties.

These enormous combines and monopolies were often highly effi-

Before the Civil War many rural Americans made nearly all they needed on their farms or at home. With industrialization, food came to be processed in great industrial centers. Instead of slaughtering an animal and salting the meat down in a barrel for future use, Americans were now buying their meat in cans, as this advertisement shows.

cient, and produced a torrent of goods, frequently at steadily dropping prices. Nonetheless, the attitude of many of the people who ran them, like the celebrated J. P. Morgan, and railroad tycoon W. H. Vanderbilt was "the public be damned," as Vanderbilt is reported to have said. The worst of them were ruthless toward competitors, their workers, and their customers as well, charging what the traffic would bear, and paying their workers just enough to keep them and their families in poverty.

To make sure that they had a free hand to do as they liked, not only the selfish but just about all managers of large businesses found ways to influence governments on all levels. In some cases they intrigued with politicians to make sure men sympathetic to the corporations ran for office. They brought pressure on congressmen to protect their privileges. Frequently they paid bribes to officials in governments low and high. (The story of these great industrialists is told in the volume in this series called *The Rise of Industry*.)

But in many cases it was not necessary for corporate giants to bribe congressmen and government officials. A great many Americans, especially middle-class Americans, who supplied most of the white-collar workers who owned the small businesses and managed the large ones, believed deeply that people had an absolute right to do whatever they wanted with their property, even when that "property" was a huge corporation employing tens of thousands of people and controlling a substantial slice of a given industry, like steel or oil. The economic system worked best, many Americans believed, when the corporations were left alone: Competition for customers' dollars would keep prices low and steadily bring about improved products.

Among those who most felt themselves damaged by the new industrial system that was spreading rapidly across the nation were the farmers of the Great Plains. They saw themselves enmeshed in a system they could not control, but which could control them. It seemed to them that the manufacturers back East were charging exorbitant prices for the things the farmers needed, like wagons, furniture, the new steel plows, and harvesters. It also seemed to them that they were frequently unable to charge enough for the wheat, beef, and wool they were producing to pay their mortgages and live in any comfort.

What the farmers and, indeed, most other working men and women of the great agricultural heartland of America could not see was their connection to the world beyond the oceans. With the coming of transoceanic steamships as well as the railroads, and telegraph lines that could transmit orders and prices for wheat, pork, and corn, the prairie farmer was dependent upon profits that were affected by prices in Australia, weather conditions in Europe, and famine in India. His market had become globalized.

Another set of intangible forces that pressed upon the farmer were those of the industrial and financial systems in America. Local banks borrowed money from the great commercial banks of New York and granted mortgages to farmers. When the big banks needed cash they pressed the small local ones, which in turn pressed the farmers. The farmers of course saw only the local banker and the local railroad agent.

In particular, it seemed to the Great Plains farmers that the railroads were cheating them to a fare-thee-well. The situation with the railroads was this: Back East the railroad network was dense, with two or more lines running into most cities and towns. Shippers had a choice, and as a consequence prices were held down to a reasonable level. Indeed, the railroads claimed that they lost money on their lines in the East. But on the vast Plains, rail lines might be a hundred miles apart. Farmers usually had no choice, but must ship on the nearby line. The railroads could charge anything they wanted, to the point where at times farmers simply could not make any profit from their produce. Making matters worse, the railroads often insisted that farmers use the railroads' own grain storage elevators. Sometimes they would classify high-quality wheat as second grade, and pay a lesser price for it. If a farmer protested, the local official would shrug and tell the farmer to take his grain elsewhere. But of course there was no elsewhere. On the other hand, many of these farmers would have still been stuck on profitless farms in New England, New York, or Germany without the support of the railroad companies and the railroad lines themselves.

One of the ways in which farmers felt abused grew out of the large grants of land the U.S. government had given the railroad companies. The companies permitted farmers to take up lands to be paid for at a certain price at a later date. This enabled poor families—many of them immigrants—to establish farms they never could have owned otherwise. Then, after the families had developed the farms, the railroad managers would raise the per acre price. Since freight rates were so high that farmers couldn't make a profit, they certainly couldn't buy their farms. Their mortgages were foreclosed, and the railroads sold the farms to richer newcomers.

A grain "elevator" was really a great storehouse where various types of wheat, corn, rye, and other grains could be kept to await shipment. Railroad companies frequently built their own grain elevators and insisted that farmers use them. This elevator belonged to the New York Central and Hudson River Railroad, and was convenient to both railroad lines and the New York City harbor from which grain was shipped in enormous quantities around the world.

Inevitably, the farmers began to fight back. It was harder for them to do so than it was for workers in the factories, for they lived distances apart, worked long hours, and could not easily gather in large groups to discuss their problems. Then, an official of the government's Agriculture Department named Oliver H. Kelley grew distressed by the bleakness and loneliness of farm life. In 1867 Kelley resigned his job and helped to form the National Grange of Patrons of Husbandry. (*Grange* was an old word, relating to grain, for farmhouse; *husband* originally meant *householder*: *husbandry* is the practice of agriculture.) The original idea of the Grange

This painting shows a meeting of Grangers in the woods near Winchester, in Scott County, Illinois. The Grange began as a social organization but soon organized politically and proved effective, for a time.

was to bring farmers and their wives together to share information about new agricultural techniques, and most importantly, to relieve their loneliness. Very quickly, however, farmers began using the rapidly spreading Grange organization to help them find ways out of their economic problems. Particularly after a depression in 1873 did the Grange sweep into action.

One of the things it tried was to organize "buying cooperatives." Such a cooperative might gather orders for a hundred plows or hay rakes from a hundred different farmers. With a large order like this the cooperative could negotiate with several manufacturers to get the best price. They found that they could get wagons for $90 instead of $150, sewing machines at half the usual price, and so on.

From the cooperatives it was a natural step for the Grange to set up its own factories to make bailers, hay rakes, and plows, and then sell the goods at cost. The already established manufacturers naturally wanted to head off this movement, and they cut the price of farm equipment down below cost, taking temporary losses until the Grange factories were forced out of business.

Losing the battle on the economic front, the Grangers turned to politics. In some states they managed to elect majorities in the legislatures. Soon states began to put into effect laws regulating prices that railroads and grain storage facilities could charge.

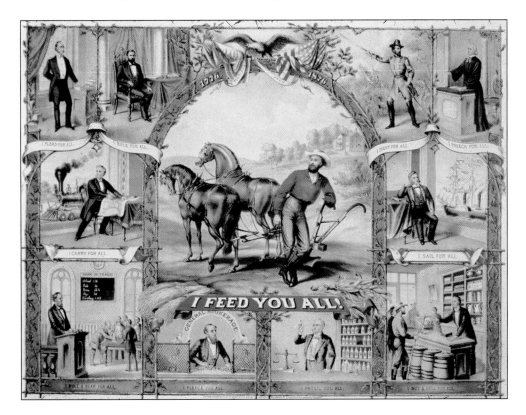

This Grange poster makes the point that farmers were feeding all other classes of workers, and ought therefore to be given a fair reward for their work, which for the most part they were not.

In a major constitutional test of these Granger Laws, an Illinois law fixing prices at storage elevators in Chicago was challenged by the elevator owners. In this case, *Munn* v. *Illinois*, the U.S. Supreme Court in 1877 upheld the Illinois law. Chief Justice Morrison R. Waite said that "when a private property is affected with a public interest," it is no longer exclusively private. The public has a right to regulate it.

However, by the mid-1880s a number of new justices had come onto the Supreme Court, most of a pro-business cast of mind. In new cases the Supreme Court reversed *Munn* v. *Illinois*, saying that states could not regulate railroad rates or control the railroads in other ways. The railroads, the Court now said, were engaged in *interstate* commerce, and could only be regulated by the federal government. But by this time it had become clear that efforts by the states to regulate great national corporations did not work, anyway. The Court only made legal what was already fact.

It was now clear that if the railroads were to be curbed it would have to be done in Washington, not the state capitals. The federal government accordingly, in 1887, passed the Interstate Commerce Act. This prohibited certain unfair practices the railroads had indulged in. Most important, it established the Interstate Commerce Commission to supervise the law. This body was the first permanent administrative board of the scores the government now has, and as such was a milestone in American history, for it clearly upheld the idea that the federal government had the right to regulate private property when it crossed state lines and involved the "public interest," a phrase that must be interpreted in the light of the facts of each individual case. Today we take it for granted that not only the federal but state governments can set minimum wages employers can pay, require companies to follow health and safety regulations, install pollution controls, and much else. Such regulation at the national level began with the Interstate Commerce Act of 1887. (The act was repealed by Congress in 1997.)

The Interstate Commerce Commission, as originally set up by the 1887 act, did not possess many teeth. The Commission could not itself force the railroads to obey its orders, but had to depend on the federal courts to enforce them, and the U.S. Supreme Court was not much inclined to limit the power of the corporations, since many of the judges themselves had been corporation lawyers. From 1887 to 1905 the Court overruled the Interstate Commerce Commission's injunctions against the railroads fifteen out of sixteen times—and then only after years—long delays during which the railroad rates and practices continued.

At the same time of those Court decisions the farmers of the Plains were hit by a series of natural disasters that finished many of them off. The early 1880s had been good years for them—as we have seen, the cattle industry peaked at that time. But then came the terrible winter of 1886–87, which was followed by ten years of drought. Farmers gave up by the thousands: According to one historian, between 1888 and 1892 half the population of western Kansas moved out, and 30,000 people left South Dakota. Thousands of farmers lost their farms to the banks, railroads, and eastern money lenders.

The basis of the problems the farmers faced was the fact that there were millions of them all competing to sell their produce, but only a few huge railroad companies—in many areas a monopoly—and giant industrial corporations that could easily coordinate their policies. Thus organization into political parties seemed to be the answer.

Conditions for the farmers continued to worsen. Now new organizations called the Farmers' Alliances decided to take action on the national level. They pulled themselves together, held a convention in 1889, and went to do battle in the elections of 1890. They scored impressive victories, winning six governorships, gaining control of several state legislatures, and electing over fifty congressmen. They decided in 1892 to form their own political party, officially known as the People's Party of the U.S.A., but now generally referred to as the People's Party or the Populists.

This party brought together not only the western farmers, but also some eastern laborers. It nominated a presidential candidate, James B. Weaver, and wrote a platform. The platform called for government ownership of the railroad tracks (but not the cars), an income tax, an eight-hour day, direct election of senators (who were at the time elected by state legislatures), and other programs then thought radical. Weaver received twenty-two electoral votes, the Republican Benjamin Harrison lost reelection, and Democrat Grover Cleveland was reelected to a second but nonconsecutive term, a unique happenstance in presidential politics.

The People's Party showed increased strength during yet another drought in 1893–94, before, as we shall see, it withered away. But not without influencing national politics in major ways by forcing attention to farmers' and westerners' concerns. As one historian has said about the party's momentary prominence, "Like a bursting bomb, Populism at once illuminated and changed the political landscape."

Grover Cleveland was hardly more sympathetic to farmers than were the Republicans. In his 1893 inaugural address he said "while the people should patriotically and cheerfully support their government, its functions do not include the support of the people." He then vetoed a congressional bill to aid drought-stricken farmers in Texas.

In 1896, though, the farmers and westerners—especially the silver-mining companies—thought their time had come. Another of the recurring economic depressions had hit the national economy, and as usual farmers bore the brunt of it. Thus one of the major issues in this campaign revolved around what is called "monetarism." This issue is too complex to explain in detail in a short space, but briefly, the problem is this:

Most farmers had mortgaged their farms, borrowed each spring to buy seed, and owed money on their new machinery. They were heavily in debt. Inflation helps debtors because while the amount of money they have to pay on their own mortgages each month stays the same, the price they receive for their produce rises. Thus, if it took a hundred bushels of wheat to make a month's payment at the time the loan was taken out, a rise in price might make only fifty bushels necessary. Unfortunately for farmers, however, the whole long period of the post–Civil War years saw farm prices *falling*, thus making it harder and harder to pay off the loans.

Businessmen, on the other hand, hate inflation. Industrialists have to know how much they can sell a product for long before it is manufactured and sold, and they must know that they can count on the stability of prices of the raw materials they must buy over the long term. Similarly, bankers don't want the money they lend to become worth less over time so that a dollar that could buy a bushel of wheat in 1880 when they lent it would only buy half of one in 1890 when it was paid back.

A fact to keep in mind is that in the period we are discussing, the U.S. government did not issue paper money; it only minted metal coins—copper, silver, and gold. Most people used coins for their daily transactions. Private banks issued paper notes that looked much like modern paper dollars for larger business needs. Debtors called for an issue of paper money like the Greenbacks temporarily circulated by the Union government during the Civil

However, not everybody agreed that farmers were not fairly rewarded for their hard work. This cartoon shows a farmer handing his mortgage to a startled Uncle Sam, making the point that farmers were trying to get the taxpayers to pay off their debts.

War. If Congress could not be persuaded to do this, then perhaps it could be persuaded to mint a lot more coins—especially silver, which was now plentiful due to the discovery of some new lodes in western states. Minting more coins could be just as inflationary as printing paper money. Grover Cleveland characterized the idea as a "dangerous and reckless experiment." Farmers and western mining companies wanted the free coinage of silver (that is, minting into coins all the silver offered for sale at a certain price); business wanted strict adherence to the gold standard—no new silver coins.

Heading into the elections of 1896 the Republicans nominated a very conservative politician, William McKinley, who was just what businessmen wanted. The Democrats came out with a platform supporting silver against gold, thus stealing the Populists' main issue. At the Democratic Convention a young delegate from Nebraska, William Jennings Bryan, made one of the most famous speeches in American history, a fiery talk that ended with the words, "You shall not press down upon the brow of labor this crown of thorns, you shall not crucify mankind upon a cross of gold." The Populists decided to join the Democrats and support Bryan. Bryan also got important support from the owners and workers in western silver mines. But the industrialists and businessmen with all their money supported McKinley, and so did most newspapers. Indeed, eastern industrial laborers, whose livelihoods depended on the success of the great corporations, also largely voted for McKinley. McKinley won; the Democrats nominated Bryan for two more unsuccessful presidential campaigns, but his inflationary programs had to wait till the Great Depression of the 1930s. (For the story of the Great Depression see the volume in this series called *The Great Depression and the New Deal*.)

Then, ironically, in the late 1890s the rains again fell on the Plains and life for the farmers got better. Conditions generally improved, farm prices went up, and for a time there was widespread prosperity. It would not last: In the 1920s bad weather and a government uninterested in the

The election of 1896 was fought out mainly over issues that were important to farmers. William Jennings Bryan was seen as a hero by the farmers. The small drawings at bottom show farmers at work, and the slogans at right say "National Prosperity, Not Trust Prosperity." A trust was a powerful business combine.

William McKinley favored high import duties, which raised the prices of goods generally, and hurt farmers who had to buy a lot of farm equipment, but protected manufacturers against foreign competition. The small buttons say "Protection," which meant high tariffs.

plight of farmers once again pushed them back into poverty, debt, and despair. But that is a story for another time.

Despite the suffering of the farmers as the good times came and went, and the depressions of 1873 and 1893 that destroyed tens of thousands of lives, the exploitation of the Great Plains by farmers and stockraisers had profound effects not just for Americans but for the world. For one thing, the realization that the Great Plains could be a source of astonishing wealth put an end to any hopes the Indians had of maintaining their own culture in any significant way.

For another, the inventive genius of Americans of that period, which threw up such a great profusion of new agricultural methods and tools, revolutionized agriculture. In the middle of the century, farmers had been working by much the same methods as they had for centuries; indeed, farming in 1830 was not in essence much different from farming at the time of the Babylonians, two thousand years before. By 1900 it was different: For many agricultural workers a farm was no longer a culture, a lifestyle; rather, they worked at a business run much like other businesses, with machines and employees, labor problems, accountants, scientific methods. Many farmers were often simply businessmen who might not even live on the farm. For many others, however, farm life continued for another generation, but by the middle of the twentieth century, only about 5 percent of Americans were farmers.

The new "agribusiness," as it is sometimes called today, was developed largely in the West, although other sections of the nation contributed. Many people lament the loss of the old family farm, with its red-painted barn, its small herd of lowing cattle in picturesque pastures, its apple orchards, kitchen gardens, sunflowers by the front door, and the woodpile behind the barn. But those were not the farms of the Great Plains, where bad times always came, the work was endless and hard, and debt was ever-present.

The modern agricultural system, developed largely in the American

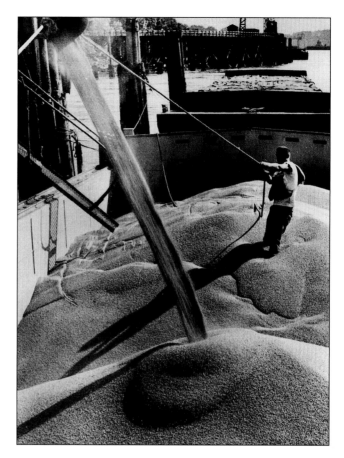

Today the enormous American agricultural system supplies food for nations around the world. Here a ship is being filled with wheat for transport to Russia in 1964. Even though the United States and Russia were on opposite sides of the Cold War then, Russia, itself a wheat-producing nation, had to buy grain from America.

West, is undoubtedly a miracle. More than people need automobiles, television sets, and computers, they need food. Possibly a third of the people living in the world as the twentieth century turned to the twenty-first are hungry; many more would be without American farm methods. Americans now sell rice to China and Japan, wheat to Russia, even wine to France in small but increasing amounts. So successful has American farming become that at the opening of the twenty-first century, only 1 percent of us feeds—indeed overfeeds—the rest of us, and feeds tens of millions of people elsewhere as well. We are not the only nation in the world with farm surpluses; many European nations especially have them, too. But Americans showed the way, and they did so to a large extent on the Great Plains. The early farmers there may have suffered a great deal; but unbeknownst to them, they wrought a miracle.

BIBLIOGRAPHY

For Teachers:

Carlson, Paul H. *The Plains Indians*. College Station: Texas A. & M. University Press, 1998.

Ewers, John C. *Plains Indians History and Culture*. Norman: University of Oklahoma Press, 1998.

Fite, Gilbert. *The Farmer's Frontier, 1865–1900*. New York: Holt, Rinehart and Winston, 1966.

Gordon, Sarah H. *Passage to Union: How the Railroads Transformed American Life, 1829–1929*. Chicago: Ivan R. Dee, 1998.

Paul, Rodman. *The Far West and the Great Plains in Transition, 1859–1900*. New York: Harper and Row, 1988.

Pollack, Norman. *The Populist Response to Industrial America*. Cambridge: Harvard University Press, 1962.

Prucha, Francis Paul. *The Great Father: The United States Government and the American Indians*. Lincoln: University of Nebraska Press, 1984.

Starrs, Paul F. *Let the Cowboy Ride: Cattle Ranching in the American West*. Baltimore: Johns Hopkins University, 1998.

Utley, Robert. *The Indian Frontier of the American West*. Albuquerque: University of New Mexico Press, 1984.

West, Elliott. *The Contested Plains: Indians, Goldseekers and the Rush to Colorado.* Lawrence: University of Kansas Press, 1998.

White, Richard. *"It's Your Misfortune and None of My Own": A New History of the American West.* Norman: University of Oklahoma Press, 1991.

For Students

Blumberg, Rhoda. *Full Steam Ahead: The Race to Build a Transcontinental Railroad.* New York: National Geographic Society, 1996.

Brown, Dee Alexander. *Bury My Heart at Wounded Knee: An Indian History of the American West.* New York: Holt, 1970. [Available in an adaptation for young readers by Amy Ehrlich, also Holt.]

DeAngelis, Gina. *The Black Cowboys.* New York: Chelsea House, 1997.

Freedman, Russell. *Children of the Wild West.* New York: Clarion Books, 1983.

———. *Cowboys of the Wild West.* New York: Clarion Books, 1985.

Jones, Mary Ellen, ed. *The American Frontier: Opposing Viewpoints.* San Diego: Greenhaven Press, 1994.

Marrin, Albert. *Cowboys, Indians, and Gunfighters: The Story of the Cattle Kingdom.* New York: Athaneum, 1993.

Press, Petra. A *Multicultural Portrait of the Move West.* Tarrytown, NY: Marshall Cavendish, 1994.

Smith, Carter, ed. *The Conquest of the West: A Sourcebook on the American West.* Brookfield, CT: Millbrook Press, 1992.

Stefoff, Rebecca. *Children of the Westward Trail.* Brookfield, CT: Millbrook Press, 1996.

Storall, TaRessa. *The Buffalo Soldiers.* New York: Chelsea House, 1997.

Time-Life Books. *Settling the West.* New York: Time-Life Books, 1996.

Wexler, Sanford, ed. *Westward Expansion: An Eyewitness History.* New York: Facts on File, 1991.

———. *An Indian Winter.* New York: Holiday House, 1992.

INDEX

Charts, graphs and illustrations are in **boldface.**

JAMES LINCOLN COLLIER is the author of a number of books both for adults and for young people, including the social history *The Rise of Selfishness in America*. He is also noted for his biographies and historical studies in the field of jazz. Together with his brother, Christopher Collier, he has written a series of award-winning historical novels for children widely used in schools, including the Newbery Honor classic, *My Brother Sam Is Dead*. A graduate of Hamilton College, he lives with his wife in New York City.

CHRISTOPHER COLLIER grew up in Fairfield County, Connecticut and attended public schools there. He graduated from Clark University in Worcester, Massachusetts and earned M.A. and Ph.D. degrees at Columbia University in New York City. After service in the Army and teaching in secondary schools for several years, Mr. Collier began teaching college in 1961. He is now Professor of History at the University of Connecticut and Connecticut State Historian. Mr. Collier has published many scholarly and popular books and articles about Connecticut and American history. With his brother, James, he is the author of nine historical novels for young adults, the best known of which is *My Brother Sam Is Dead*. He lives with his wife Bonnie, a librarian, in Orange, Connecticut.